# MUSICAL INSTRUMENTS

Johannes Rademacher

**BARRON'S**

**Cover photos from top to bottom and left to right:**
Miniature in the manuscript of the *Liber viaticus* by Johannes von Neumarkt, 14th century /
Leonard Bernstein, photo dpa / Wall painting in an Etruscan tomb, Werner Dausien Verlag,
Hanau / Trumpet player / L.C. de Carmontelle, "Wolfgang Amadeus Mozart and his Father
Leopold" / Anne-Sophie Mutter, photo dpa / Baryton built by Joachim Tielke, Hamburg, 1686,
Victoria and Albert Museum, London / Steelband, Kingstown, photo Bernhard Wagner,
Leinfelden / Organ, photo J.E. Hysek, Prague / Egyptian wall painting, Werner Dausien Verlag,
Hanau / An Indian string instrument called Tayuc, Naprstek Museum, Prague / Elvis Presley
**Back cover photos from top to bottom:**
Johannes Kupezky (1667?–1740), "The Flute Player", Hungarian National Museum, Budapest
/ Hungarian hurdy-gurdy, Werner Dausien Verlag, Hanau / Orff instruments, Studio 49
Musikinstrumentenbau GmbH, Gräfelfing
**Background:**
Johann Sebastian Bach, "Partita II for solo violin in d minor, Staatsbibliothek zu Berlin,
Preußischer Kulturbesitz, Musikabteilung
**Frontispiece:**
"The 24 Oldes Men", miniature in a manuscript by Heinrich Czuns, 1448, Landesbibliothek
Coburg

American text version by: Editorial Office Sulzer-Reichel, Rösrath, Germany
Translated by: Ann Jeffers-Brown, Cambridge, Mass. and
              Sally Schreiber, Friedrichshafen, Germany
Edited by: Bessie Blum, Cambridge, Mass.

First edition for the United States and Canada
published by Barron's Educational Series, Inc., 1997.

First published in the Federal Republic of Germany in 1996 by
DuMont Buchverlag GmbH und Co. Kommanditgesellschaft, Köln.

Text copyright © 1996 DuMont Buchverlag GmbH und Co. Kommanditgesellschaft,
Köln, Federal Republic of Germany.

Copyright © 1997 U.S. language translation, Barron's Educational Series, Inc.

*All inquiries should be addressed to:*
Barron's Educational Series, Inc.
250 Wireless Boulevard
Hauppauge, New York 11788

Library of Congress Catalog Card No. 96-78858

ISBN  0-7641-0052-1

Printed in Italy by Editoriale Libraria

# Contents

# Preface

The variety of musical instruments found in a society has a lot to say to the alert observer and listener: Instruments reflect the entire culture—a way of life and a way of thinking—as well as the role of music and art and literature in the life of the people.

The significance of musical instruments and the roles they assume within the cultures of the world are quite diverse. In some non-Western cultures, musical instruments are embued with magical or healing power, while in many an affluent Western culture, an instrument—say, a Steinway grand piano—may serve as a decorative centerpiece in the living room of someone who doesn't know how to play. Thus, any attempt we make to comprehend musical instruments brings us face to face with a tremendous range of kinds of instruments which, in turn, can serve dissimilar purposes and have considerably different meanings for the social contexts in which they are found.

As with many elements of any heterogeneous culture such as that of western Europe, the historical development of musical instruments was continually swayed by external influences. This development may well be considered complete: No completely new instruments are likely to be invented. Electronic instruments may acquire ever new synthetic sounds, they may come in different packages (smaller and more accessible to the average computer user or popular consumer), but their nature and construction will remain essentially the same as before.

In the course of history, the social significance of musical instruments has changed a great deal. Only a few instruments—for example, the role of the church organ in the sacred domain—have maintained a static social position. On the other hand, various musical experiments—such as performances utilizing original period instruments or the integration of exotic instruments into commercial ethno-pop—have altered our very perceptions of what music is or can be.

The focus of this book, which draws its examples primarily from the Western European traditions, while also looking at instruments of interest from other parts of the world, is on the construction of musical instruments, their historical development, the techniques by which they are played, and the repertoires composed or collected for them.

Johannes Rademacher, Köln

## The origin of the instruments

The vast profusion of musical instruments, their manifold forms and, naturally, their almost endless ability to produce sounds of various kinds have long fascinated people around the world. And just as richly varied as the instruments themselves are the meanings they embody for musicians, critics, historians, theorists, philosophers, and sociologists. This variety also intrigues listeners, whose relation with music is more passive—that is, whose contact with the instruments themselves consists of attending a concert or listening to the radio or a compact disc.

The particular appeal of musical instruments is probably due to the fact that, as cultural products, they are not merely vessels for expressing a certain intellectual perspective, but in fact are the direct means for conveying one of life's most elementary emotional and sensual experiences (**2**). A musical instrument is both an aid (Lat. *instrumentum*) in the production of sound and at the same time a reflection of the cultural understanding of a given time and milieu. It is this dual nature that makes instruments so indispensable and attracts our most serious attention.

1 The Australian aboriginal didjeridoo is one of the world's oldest instruments. The tube is blown like a trumpet, producing a muffled tone capable of great modulation. Didjeridoo players are able to produce continuous tones by a special kind of sustained breathing. The tones can be greatly varied. Above the bourdon, or droning, the player adds sung melodies, thus producing extremely complex musical structures.

## Musical instruments— Models and forms

Every object suited to the production of sound can be used as a musical instrument. Even our hands serve as an instrument, in a narrow sense—when we arch our palms and

clap our hands together or, on a somewhat more complicated level, when a clogger or a Morris dancer claps them against various parts of the body. The human body finds it almost as irresistible to clap as to move—to dance—when we listen to music, especially vocal music containing strong rhythmic elements. What probably springs to mind in this regard are gospel songs or spirituals—and much of the music that grew from these traditions—which move the listener on many levels—their rhythms are so infectious that an audience is readily drawn into rhythmic clapping or finger-snapping.

From this basic music-making activity, it is but a small step to taking two blocks of wood—which, when clapped against each other, make a distinctly different sound than that of clapping hands—and transforming them into a musical instrument. Watch a small child at play and you will see how basic a part of human nature this process is.

**2** Music plays an important part in the social life of virtually every culture in the world. For example, the many grave paintings illustrating musical activity suggest that music was highly valued in ancient Egypt. The form of musical instruments is similar throughout the Mediterranean region: To the left of the dancer, the seated woman plays a wind instrument resembling the Greek aulos; next to her is a woman playing cymbals.

**3** One of the earliest wind instruments is the flute made of hollow animal bones. Even early instruments had finger holes to alter the pitch and tone produced.

**4** Rock paintings often depict men hunting—and hunting bows can easily be used as musical instruments ...

## New functions for an everyday object

Attempts to explain how musical instruments came into existence are just as multifarious as the forms of the instruments themselves. One fairly sobering but enlightening explanation is that many early utensils were used in so many different ways that yet additional ideas for their application were inevitable. Often, it was not even necessary to alter the construction of a tool to render it fit as a musical instrument.

The multiple functions of the hunting bow, known since the earliest days of human history, are particularly obvious (**4**). Whether or not the bow really came into use simultaneously for hunting and music making remains open to conjecture, but the idea is quite plausible (**5**). We can see this very process in action today: Folk musicians, certain ethnic-music ensembles, percussionists, and jug bands simply adapt household items to be used along with their traditional instruments. Concave spoons can become a regular virtuoso rhythm instrument and, as in the 1930s, even the ordinary washboard can be used to produce an ordered sequence of sounds.

In the 1960s and 1970s, when the folk music revival was more or less at its peak, it was common to spot a washboard player among the entertainers on street corners and in subway stations. Sometimes the washboard is not played with bare hands but with thimbles, which amplifies the sound (along with the reverberating acoustics of the cavernous subways) and spares the fingertips! In

**5** ... as seen in this South African rock painting.

effect, the transformation of the washboard into a musical instrument entails using yet other objects from other realms of practical utility. This simple development—from the fingertip to the thimble—may well be just a first step in this instrument's further—and theoretically endless—development.

## Signals, information, and messages

While the relatively simple process of transforming everyday objects into musical instruments is fascinating to observe, we may also look into the instruments' historical roots to discover the conscious development, or discovery, of a sound-producing apparatus specifically intended to convey information (6). Lacking satellites and fiber-optics for long-distance communication, early cultures found their own ways to relay messages, even though the limitations of the means may well have curbed the nature and amount of data exchange, as we are used to thinking of communication today.

6 One of the earliest functions of musical instruments was to transmit a signal. A horn, which can be heard from a great distance, allows information to be spread easily.

Many African cultures used drums with tonal differences capable of communicating quite complex messages. Europeans also offer vivid examples of the same sorts of applications: The Swiss alpenhorn (7), audible across great distances, makes it possible to send information

7 The alpenhorn gives tourists an impression of the traditional world of the mountains. Alpine shepherds originally used the alpenhorn to "converse" across the mountains and valleys.

8   Church bells retain their function as a means of communication. They call congregations to services and mark the hours. Mechanical forms of bells can also be used musically to produce complex melodic and rhythmic structures. In the 18th century, the carillon, a set of stationary bells, had two or three octaves, while 20th-century instruments may have as many as six.

without much ado *and* makes music. In the alpine region we can also find cow bells, which not only tell the cowherd where to find his own herd but also let him know if any stray "foreign" cows wander into his fields. The cow bell thus allows the cowherd to mark his territory and becomes expressive of a sense of native soil and homeland.

The extent to which bells of various kinds may transcend their function as mere signals and enter the realm of magical or spiritual meaning becomes clear when, for example, church bells (8) call a congregation to prayer, herald a wedding ceremony, warn of the dangers of fire, floods, and storms, and announce something as conceptual as the passage of time.

## Musical instruments and spiritualism

As with music itself, many cultures believe that musical instruments bear a special relationship to supernatural forces, gods, spirits, and demons. Even the so-called developed cultures of the western hemisphere embue the music produced by certain instruments with a particular psychic effect, although the connection with the religious or spiritual sphere may be tenuous. There is generally a strong connection in most cultures

9   An angel plays a portative, a small organ of treble flue pipes whose bellows are worked by hand. This picture shows almost all the medieval instruments except for the various kinds of drums, which were considered unfit to be played upon or depicted.

between spiritual or religious beliefs and practices and the sounds and uses of its musical instruments.

Historically, this has been a ripe and galvanizing topic among scholars and musicians of various cultures, who have tried to determine and regulate an instrument's value and stature within a given culture.

10 The Semitic lyre. Grave painting from Beni Hasan, Egypt, ca. 1920–1900 BC.

11 A reconstructed Sumerian lyre from a grave site in Uruk (Iraq), ca. 2700–2500 BC. The musical instrument aficionado is always interested in restoring the artifacts of old cultures visually and, if possible, audibly. Reproductions of old instruments based on pictorial and/or descriptive records can serve the same purpose.

### Forms, terms of reference, organization

In all of the ancient classical cultures whose music and instruments are in any way known to us, there were many different views about the properties that combine to make a musical instrument. The Sumerians gave instruments double-barreled names, as it were: One term described the material—reed, wood, leather, skin, or metal—while a second word designated the instrument's ritualistic function. One instrument that served a ritualistic purpose is the Sumerian lyre. In Mesopotamia, the bull was honored as a sacred animal; Sumerian priests, thus, accompanied their hymns with a lyre in the shape of a bull in the belief that the bull form would help the gods understand their prayers (11).

In ancient Greece, musical instruments were esteemed as highly as the music produced on

**12** An aulos player. Detail on a Greek vase painting, 5th century BC. Like the aulos, double oboes were common throughout the Mediterranean region.

**13** Egyptian women playing a harp and a double oboe. Wall painting in a grave in the necropolis at Thebes, New Kingdom, 1435–1405 BC.

them (**12**). Not only was music known to have an effect on the listener's psyche, it was also commonly believed that music had a special power to create and maintain man's relations with the gods.

From the start, the distinction and classification of instruments according to their form seems to have been empirically based and quite objective. The name "aulos" for the wind instrument with two blowing tubes derives naturally from the word for pipes (**14**). Similarly, the names for the most important instruments of ancient Greece, the kithara and the lyre (**10**), refer to their external form. Originally the lyre's soundchest was made from—or in the shape of—a tortoise-shell, while the somewhat larger kithara was made of wood, and drawn with strings.

In striking contrast to this objective approach are classification systems that distinguish between "inspired" and "uninspired" instruments or that suggest an instrument's ability to produce a continuous tone. Such methods of classification preclude any possibility of drawing a clear boundary between types of instruments. The Greeks, however, were apparently unfazed by such limitations; they did not consider such distinctions particularly important. For the ancient Greeks, a continuous tone was a symbol of eternity—and whether it was produced by a wind or a string instrument scarcely mattered.

## Medieval perspectives

The European scholars of the Middle Ages took an approach quite similar to those of the ancients. Fundamentally indifferent about clear categories

14 Etruscan aulos and barbiton (right) players. The barbiton is a special type of lyre.

and distinctions, they were more centrally concerned with whether and how an instrument was suited for their religious services. In short, while both the instruments and music, as well as the religious practice and liturgy, may have differed from those of the ancients, in both cultures music served a spiritual purpose which took precedence over any method of producing sound.

This return to classical distinctions (15) implies that the instruments assumed an ethical or moral dimension. By classifying instruments according

PITAGORAS

to whether they were inspired or uninspired, whether they produced a "natural" or an "artificial" tone, those with an interest in drawing such distinctions were able to distinguish between wind and string instruments—although the categorical divisions remained rather vague. The connection, common in the medieval imagination, between breath and spirit remains with us today.

15 The model for the medieval music theorist: the Greek mathematician and philosopher Pythagoras.

**16** Piping music in small groups might have appeared like this in Virdung's day. Many wind instruments are quite loud, lending themselves to open-air performance.

**17** In Anjou, France, a miniaturist portrays music as an allegory and illustrates the typical instruments used by troubadors, trouvers, and minnesingers. Virdung's hated drums were a very popular and natural component in the music of medieval France.

### *"Musica getutscht ..."*

In 1511, the German music theorist and composer Sebastian Virdung of Basel published *Musica getutscht und ausgezogen*, which may be roughly translated as "Music explained in the German language." Virdung was the first theoretician who concentrated explicitly on instruments: His treatise attempts a classification of instruments and discusses notation; it does not particularly draw upon the philosophical context or consider the instruments' social standing.

While Virdung's early manual occasionally reveals the author indulging in some crass judgments regarding which instruments are appropriate for church music and which are suitable only for folk music, he nonetheless proceeds from a fairly comparative and analytic position. He divides instruments into three groups: "those that are drawn with strings," those "made of hollow tubes ... blown with wind," and "those made from metal or other clinking material."

With no apparent concern, Virdung manages to ignore the entire range of percussion instruments. We might be shocked by such an omission, were it not for the author's own bold explanation that "all drums do the same—they cause great disturbance ... to invalids and the ill, to those meditating in the cloisters, and those who must read and study and pray; and I believe and

hold it for truth that the devil dreamed up and made [these instruments], for absolutely no beauty or goodness is in them, but rather a suppression of all sweet melodies and music as a whole." Virdung shows a touch of prescience concerning the effect of these instruments: Today many percussion instruments are used by music

therapists, though not because they "cause great disturbance," for working with "invalids and the ill."

### The variety of strings

As thoroughly as Virdung condemned and slighted percussion instruments as the devil's works, so he gave countervailing attention to string instruments. To him, not only did strings produce the essence of harmony but, unlike those satanic percussives, they were the expression of divine harmony. He divided the string instruments in use at the beginning of the 16th century into four groups:

1. *Instruments with keys.* These included the clavichord, the harpsichord, and the vielle, or hurdy-gurdy (**18**).
2. *Instruments with a chordal string arrangement and frets:* These included the lute and the viola da gamba (**19**).
3. *Many-stringed instruments:* Among these are the harp, the dulcimer, and the psaltery (**20**).
4. *Instruments with few strings and no frets.*

The last group, which contained the "smaller violins" ("die cleyn gei-

18   Vielle, or hurdy-gurdy, player. Painting by George de la Tour (1593–1652).

19   Lute player.

20   Psaltery.

**21**   This miniature from the *Cantigas de Santa Maria* of the Spanish king Alphonse the Wise depicts two string instrument players.

gen") Virdung described as "useless instruments." Often, as in Virdung's dismissal of the very instruments that came to dominate western music, his assessments may offer very little insight beyond his driving motive to fit all instruments into a system akin to a divine order, and this divine order needed to accommodate not only all instruments but all aspects of life during his time.

To divide up instruments according to the mechanics of their tone pro-

duction is an arbitrary process. Virdung assigned all keyed instruments to a single classification, while he distinguished among string instruments both according to the number, organization, and chordal relationships of the strings, and according to whether or not the instrument had frets. There is little doubt that this classification system was burdened with a moral dimension that corresponded to the social values assigned to the instruments in general. Soon after its invention, the harpsichord (**22**)—a keyboard instru-

**22**
Because of its form and string-plucking mechanism, the harpsichord was also known as a quill clavier.

**23**   The clavichord held a fairly high place in Virdung's estimation because of its ability to produce harmonies.

ment whose strings are plucked by quills rather than tapped by a hammer—became an indispensable element of the musical activity of both the nobility and the bourgeoisie; within two hundred years, owning a harpsichord became a regular status symbol. The clavichord (**23**), on the other hand, where the strings are struck by a small metal hammer to produce an extraordinarily light tone, did not enjoy the same popular prestige as the harpsichord; for Virdung, however, it was superior to the harpsichord because of its better ability to create harmony.

The lute and viola da gamba—the former plucked, the latter stroked with a bow—can also produce harmony, and thus were rated higher by Virdung than instruments that normally produced only melody. Virdung counted harps, dulcimers, and the medieval psaltery as kinds of lutes. At the low end of his scale were the fretless instruments with few strings.

Thus, back in 1511 when Virdung's book appeared, the violin (**25**) was still a lower-class instrument, played at annual markets, fairs, and in inns. A mere two centuries, however, overturned this instrumental hierarchy and the violin became

**24** Players of reed instruments and cornets from the *Cantigas de Santa Maria.*

**25** Early forms of the violin.

**26** Michael Praetorius was a composer as well as an influential theorist. *Terpischore*, his collection of dances, is well known and still popular today among recorder players.

**27** This illustration from *De Organographia* shows various gambas.

one of the leading instruments in ensembles and orchestras: There would be no more talk of a "useless instrument."

## "Whatever instruments can be blown"

Virdung divided the majority of wind instruments into those blown directly by the player and those that used a bellows. In his system, the level of human involvement was more important than the technique of tone production. For this reason, Virdung ranked wind instruments with finger holes higher than those without them. To the Renaissance scholar, whose primary interest lay in the significance of human activity, this system had its justification, however arbitrary it may seem today.

### *De Organographia*

One century later, in 1619, another German theorist/composer, Michael Praetorius (**26**), published his survey of musical instruments, *De Organographia*, as the second volume in his music encyclopedia, *Syntagma musicum*. A hundred years had wrought no significant changes in how instruments were regarded. Unlike his predecessor Virdung, however, Praetorius was not selective in his survey of instruments, but rather endeavored to include all the instruments of his time. While Praetorius refrained from the sort of ideological valuation that demonized and ignored entire classes of instruments, his groupings, too, were quite irregular at times.

Praetorius distinguished between two main groups:

the "inflata, piping instruments or those into or out of which air is blown," and the "percata, striking instruments." While this at first glance might raise an eyebrow, and make us wonder what happened to all the strings, our concern is mollified by his rationale for including the strings within the category of struck instruments: "And there are those [instruments] which are struck with special wooden objects or other things."

### Inflatilia, or instruments that are blown

For Praetorius's schema, the mechanism by which air was delivered to an instrument was critical. His key criterion was whether the air was produced by breath or with a bellows—although, acoustically, the two constitute the same process. From this perspective, the organ (28) assumed an unexpectedly special importance, which, by more modern standards, it does not really deserve. It's quite likely that Praetorius, conscious of the organ's significance for society (via its religious application), considered it

**28** Organs come in a wide range of sizes and shapes. This instrument was meant for making music at home.

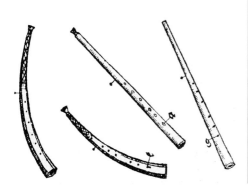

**29** Straight and curved cornets from the *Syntagma musicum* by Michael Praetorius. Cornets can be played with great virtuosity. Like trumpets, they have rounded mouthpieces, but they produce a light and clear tone.

21

**30** The combination of so-called hand drums with wind instruments, still popular in Spain and southern France, was already evident in the time of King Alphonse the Wise, as this miniature shows.

necessary to assign this instrument a category of its own.

Praetorius's distinctions among the "true" wind instruments, on the other hand, rested entirely on how they were played. Classification was based on whether the player produced a tone solely through blowing into the instrument, as with some horns, or whether the production of a tone required some further activity on the part of the player, such as closing the finger holes on flutes, cornets (**29**), and oboes, or moving the slide on a trombone.

### Fidicinia—Struck, stroked, plucked

The category of the *percussa* is particularly lacking in organization; on the whole, however, instruments are categorized according to the manner in which a sound is produced. Thus, for example, Praetorius lumped together drums, triangles, and xylophones because they are all sounded "by means of iron or wooden mallets or sticks" (**30**).

His process of classifying instruments where strings are struck is similar. The defining factor was how the sound was produced: by stroking with a bow on the violin or gamba strings (**31**) or by a resin-coated wheel in a hurdy-gurdy; by plucking with the naked finger on a lute or by plucking with a plectrum (or pick) or a quill on a harpsichord.

**31** Violins were originally the instruments of choice for popular dance accompaniment.

Praetorius followed another principle of observation when he distinguished instruments according to whether they emitted a steady tone or a tone that could be varied by the player. Thus, he also considered formulating a classificatory schema based on whether an instrument was

# Grouping by Threes

capable of producing many tones or only simple melodies.

**Grouping by threes**

Although Praetorius posited only two groups, it will be obvious to any reader of the *De Organographia* that the organization of instruments according to the striking of strings or other parts of the instruments was not sustainable.

In 1636–37, the French mathematician, philosopher, and theorist Marin Mersenne took another tack in his *Harmonie universelle* (**32**), although he too consigned the organ to a special category because of its complexity. His point of departure remained a classification into three groups: instruments that are blown, instruments that are struck, and instruments that produce sound by means of strings.

The German polyhistorian, theologian, and music theorist Athanasius Kircher, in his 1650 work *Musurgia universalis*, also maintained a

Historical Overview

**32** Marin Mersenne, *Harmonie universelle*. Title page of the French instruction book of music theory.

**33** Eventually, the orchestra acquired a standard format.

**34** Saxophones, invented by the Belgian wind-instrument maker Adolphe Sax, were constructed for use in military orchestras. They are basically a development of the clarinet.

**35** The giraffe piano is a particularly curious, and rather rare, form of the upright piano.

three-pronged division, with the organ classified among the wind-powered instruments.

## Names, terms, curiosities

Little new thought was expended on the organization, relationships, and building principles of musical instruments during the next two centuries. Instruments were improved, developed, and to some extent reinvented, but their description remained confusing and interest in a systematic organization was slight. However, at a time when orchestras were becoming stable ensembles in Europe (**33**), and orchestral sections were beginning to assume standardized positions, this confusion over the typology of instruments had some disastrous ramifications as erroneous designations and classifications, many of which told virtually nothing about an instrument, lingered and flourished in the minds of musicians and audiences. Thus, for example, orchestra members, composers, and conductors still classified the entirely metallic transverse flute as a wooden wind instrument, just as it had been denominated during the baroque and early classical periods.

Of course, it is easy to make note of a few misnomers and cast them into definitive, preexisting instrumental categories when we have the advantage of a historical perspective on the designations. Thus, the saxophone (**34**), originally used for military music, was placed in the orchestra among the woodwind instruments because its mouthpiece was similar to that of a clarinet.

With newly invented or less common instruments, classification becomes more complicated. Where an external characteristic is at issue—for example, in the arrangement of strings on the body of an instrument that looks from a distance like a giraffe—then a designation that draws on that characteristic may be appropriate—the designation "giraffe piano" (**35**) seems suitable, even though the instrument has nothing to do with giraffes. Equally meaningless from a musical perspective—but at the same time easily understood—is the term *pochette*, for the pocket violin or kit fiddle whose small sound box allows it to be stuffed comfortably into a pocket (**36**).

For instruments from non-European cultures, classification was at first utterly chaotic and subject to chance and whim. Initially, the interest in these so-called nontraditional instruments was purely scholastic—aimed merely at producing a complete catalogue and

**36**  The kit or pocket fiddle was much easier for traveling musicians to carry. Because of its small sound box, its tone was rather poor, but penetrating, and certainly usable for a dance master's purposes.

**37**  The mbimba is an African instrument that made its way to Europe in colonial times. Instruments of this kind can be found in almost every ethnic-music shop.

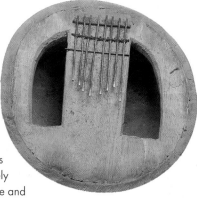

archive for storage or display in museums. Many an instrument was assigned a name totally arbitrarily, with little regard for the name's meaning or utility, while the instrument itself was labeled and returned to its shelf, where, untouched and unplayed, it remained.

Such was the fate of the non-western musical instruments until the end of the 19th century, when their importance as expressions of a civilization, and not as mere colonial goods (37), began to be appreciated, just as art from non-western cultures—from Africa, Oceania, South America, and the "Orient"—began to generate interest in the European and American cultural capitals. Only then did a system arise that was both comprehensive enough to take into account all the instruments of the world and empirically secure enough to satisfy this global requirement.

## Observation and description

Two factors were critical for the quality of a comprehensive system: It must be verifiable and intelligible. In other words,

**38, 39**  It is thanks to collectors and curators of folk art and folklore museums that the western cultures came to appreciate and respect musical instruments as cultural artifacts. Most of the pieces in such collections were acquired during the periods of colonization. Above: a Japanese instrument called a bianchin, which is a type of glockenspiel. Left: an Indian string instrument called a tayuc.

the organizing criteria of the system cannot be grounded in ideology, as they were for Sebastian Virdung, who considered drums satanic in origin and therefore not worth thinking about. Further-

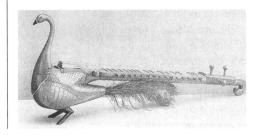

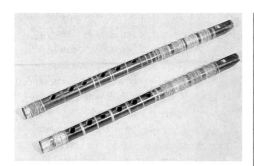

40   Pakistani bansor flutes.

more, a way had to be found to operate methodically and uniformly in order to describe all instruments, both the well known and the unknown, to assess them, and finally also to understand them.

An idea for just such a system was provided by Victor-Charles Mahillon (1841 – 1924), the son of a family of Belgian wind instrument makers. Mahillon was curator of the Brussels Conservatory Instrumental Museum which housed a vast collection of instruments, including many from the former Belgian colonies in Africa. Mahillon, a renowned acoustician, proceeded from the assumption that sound could be produced—that is, air could be set in motion by an instrument—in only four possible ways:

41   A hand drum and a horn can be played together by a single musician.

—A vibrating string moves the air.
—A closed column of air is moved to vibrate.
—A tight skin emits vibrations into the surrounding air.
—A solid but sufficiently elastic body vibrates and produces air waves.

This acoustical method of observation distinguishes instruments according to a single criterion—namely, by the physical production of sound. And so Mahillon inspired and at the same time laid the groundwork for further reflections on creating a comprehensive and reliable system of classifying musical instruments.

**42** Playing music before a home audience can be a pleasure or a burden for young children.

## Teaching and learning

Many cultural activities resemble speaking or singing: They are forms of communication learned simply by listening, watching, and imitating—the so-called mother tongue method. It is possible to learn a foreign language by repetition and imitation without knowing anything about phonetic patterns or grammatical relationships. Scientists have even demonstrated that exposure to the sounds of different languages (and to music) in the first years of life actually trains the brain to understand such sounds as meaningful, and sets in motion a certain capacity in the individual mind. A language can be picked up by listening to foreign radio programs or watching foreign television stations. Normally this kind of learning is incomplete but it at least introduces one to a language: Literacy and more formalized teaching may come later to develop what we call fluency and a deeper degree of knowledge.

To develop a higher level of fluency and literacy, however—except for the exceptional, occasional genius—learning needs to be a process of communication. The individual needs more than exposure; he or she needs a teacher, especially for learning the more formalized aspects of any language.

Music is also a language. Learning to play a musical instrument has a lot in common with learning a language. By observing a musician, one can become familiar with certain technical basics. At some point, however (though, again, we ought to note that there are exceptions to this rule), only the active exchange between teacher and student—an exchange that can range from conveying technical details to discussions of musical aesthetics—will instill certain essential elements of music making that elude the self-taught. And even the so-called self-taught will at some point gravitate toward others who can teach them more than they can achieve on their own. To exaggerate a bit, only then will the process move appreciably from "Chopsticks" to Haydn or Chopin.

## Instruments for producing noises

Of course, it is easy enought to play an instrument designed only to generate noise. With no help from a teacher or written directions, one's very first attempts bring about the desired results and most likely exhaust the possibilities of the instrument (though not the player, who may yet learn to shape those sounds into distinct rhythmic patterns). Many idiophones—rattles or chimes or other simple devices that jangle or click (**43**)—are among the easily-learned instruments. On the other hand, idiophones such as the Spanish castanets demand real expertise.

## Autodidactic instruments

In addition to instruments that can be played with virtually no practice, there are some for which at least some practice and technique is required for proficiency. Through self-study, combined with a modicum of joy in experimentation, one can become acquainted in short order with the full range of musical possibilities of these instruments and become an adept player. For example, the actual "playing" of a washboard with thimble-capped fingers is easy. There is no particular "proper position" for holding the instrument—whatever feels right is right—and technique has little bearing on the quality of sound produced. Another such rudimentary and simple instrument to play is the kazoo, which is mostly considered a child's instru-ment, though it has been used for special effects in some recorded (and presumably live) music, as in jug bands and ethnic, folk, or comic pop music. The kazoo generates a raspy sort of humming sound when one sings into it: the sound of the voice vibrates against a thin membrane. The simplest version of the kazoo is a comb with a piece of parchment drawn over it. Clearly, it does not require many lessons to be able to play it masterfully.

## First lessons: Early education

There are about as many systems of early childhood musical instruction as there are cultures and societies throughout the world, if not far more. These systems range from highly formalized and rigidly pre-

**43** To play such a rattle requires no prior musical knowledge. Turning the wheel produces a rasping noise that carries over a long distance.

# Music Education

scribed programs to development-
ally progressive programs to individual, tribal, and familial traditions.
A question facing many parents,
educators, and music teachers is
how do we introduce our children to
music? Do we just play lots of music
for them, sing to them, take them to
concerts, and if we do, what kind of
music do we expose them to and do
we intercede in their appreciation in
some way? Or do we attempt something more formal, and if so, when
and how?

Some very early childhood programs such as Dalcroze eurhythmics
introduce musical concepts while
training children's ears through progressive combinations of movements, story telling, percussion, and
clapping exercises, eventually leading into simple notation and keyboard geography. Only later may a
child learn to play a particular
instrument.

### Monkey see, monkey do

In contrast, the "talent education"
system of the Suzuki method starts
the child off playing proportionally
smaller violins. The "student" must

**44** Schleffele, a Swiss version of castanets.

listen daily to a tape or CD of the
music he or she is learning to play in
order to absorb its rhythm, intonation
and melody on an intuitive level.
Later, the child learns to read notes,
and flute or piano training, for example, is delayed until the child can
better control its breath and spread
its fingers. Under the Suzuki method,
many a three-year-old
began her playing
career on a 16th-size
violin that looks like a

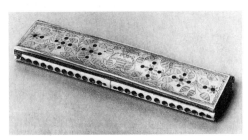

**45** Harmonica playing is
technically easy. The mouth
harmonica hardly has the
reputation of a virtuoso
instrument—but it can be played
like one!

doll's instrument, but has progressed to play Bach minuets. Dr. Suzuki called his technique the "mother tongue" method of learning. In many cultures throughout the world, imitation

**47** Ensemble playing has always offered a particularly fine experience of community and fellowship—as is evident in this 1656 painting by Jacob van Velsen.

is the self-evident prerequisite to learning an instrument or singing. Supposedly Jerry Lee Lewis learned to play the stride and boogie-woogie piano by sneaking into gin joints. Such knowledge and its transmission is an essentially "oral" tradition where the "student" learns to replicate the content, form, and style of the teacher.

**46** The concertina is also easy to learn. Two different notes are sounded when the player presses one of the buttons and either pushes or pulls on the bellows. The sobriquet "squeeze box" may sound rather derogatory, but is nonetheless descriptive and is used in many areas to designate both this instrument and the accordion, which has a keybord in place of the buttons.

## Group playing

Instruments with assigned tone frequencies and those played with mallets or sticks (such as xylophones) offer easy access to both music itself and the benefits of co-operative playing. Learning to play music together is an important aspect of a child's early musical education, and at some point, some degree of ensemble playing is usually introduced—whether in small chamber groups, beginning orchestras, choral groups, or even in a manner as simple as a duet played on a piano. The ensemble (notably, a constituent part of Suzuki training) develops the child's timing, intonation, rhythm, and, in the best of all possible worlds, sense of enjoyment derived from music when it assumes a social dimension. Ensemble playing conveys direct and concrete insight into the

**48** In our culture, music is taught chiefly through music "pieces" which give the player exact instructions for performance. The numbers above the base line of this violin sonata tell the basso continuoso instrumentalist which tones of the given chord he or she is to play. Normally an organ, a harpsichord, or possibly a lute, provides the continuoso.

structures and orderly unfolding of the music.

The teacher's role in early childhood musical education can be quite varied, and indelibly significant. A teacher can, simply, make or break a child's lifelong relationship with music. A teacher who maintains institutionally imposed constraints on both method and content can dampen a child's natural abilities and creativity, while one who can reach children thoughtfully and intelligently can not only ease the pedagogical path but serve as a role model for the rest of the child's life.

## Music in the schools

For many, music education means little more than singing a popular song or nursery rhyme, while for others, it may be interdisciplinary, encompassing music and social history. Many secondary schools have a band or orchestra, but they vary greatly in style and ability.

Based on the longstanding success and fame of New York City's High School of Music, which boasts a first-rate orchestra and a variety of ensembles as well as a thorough education for its music "majors" and supplementary courses for its "minors," many public school systems have established "emphasis" schools which require a musical audition for entry. But on the whole, the standards of public music education and school

**49** Autograph of the "Moonlight Sonata." Every piano student attempts this Beethoven sonata. Musicality can carry the player through the first two movements but the last requires a great deal of practice.

orchestras remain unpredictable. Too often, ensemble playing is characterized by the group's weakest members, all the more so since the stronger players are often drained off to either private or public special schools. To compensate for this unpredictable quality, many school ensembles rely upon a repertoire of non-threatening pieces that are more easily "mastered." Baroque music is a common choice, but while the baroque corpus is large, there is a boring tendency to stick to pieces that are all on a single level because they are eminently playable. The same syndrome occurs with even modern orchestral selections. However, a more dynamic music teacher may attempt the *Concerti grossi* of George Frederick Handel or Arcangelo Corelli.

Normally the school program must be augmented with outside

50 Clifford Curzon's entries on his working score of W.A. Mozart's "Piano Concert in D Minor" (KV 466). For a musician, this kind of intensive analysis (which, as here, can be carried out in writing) is a matter of course.

instruction if a student is to advance in technique, ear-training and style. Such privately trained students may enhance the school's orchestra, but it is unlikely that an average school setting can do more than extend the students'

51 One of the favorite forms of musical performance is the private concert. Usually the public is not terribly demanding and simply wants to be entertained. In class recitals at a conservatory, on the other hand, the quality of the musicianship is very much an issue.

**52** A sarangi player. This Indian string instrument accompanies a melody or lead by paraphrasing it. The music student learns not only the technique of playing, but also composition, through imitation. The sarangi, however, is played only in support of the lead.

exposure to music, convey fundamental theory, and provide the experience of collaborative music-making.

## Individual instruction

In private, and usually individual, instrumental instruction, the approach, character, style, and ability of the music teacher become a driving force in the student's musical education. The truly skilled or gifted instructor can work with the child's own natural inclinations, tastes, and temperament, while fulfilling all the requisites of teaching technique, theory, and repertoire. The actual repertoire taught can be drawn from almost any era: A piano student may well find it more useful at times to learn the blues than a Bach invention; both may teach the student about structure and expand his or her musical knowledge.

Individual instrumental instruction is not justified on the basis of producing concertmasters or prima donnas, but by the value of musical education in any individual's life.

## Music conservatories

It is the job of the conservatory, or the music academy, to develop musical ability above and beyond the education offered by public schools or programs, or private instructors. Here instruction concentrates on teaching students not only to interpret musical compositions, but to grapple with them intellectually. This is the basis of the profession of the music teacher and the orchestral musician.

The conservatory should offer more than a theoretic approach to music study. Technical mastery depends on maintaining the agility of whichever parts of one's body are involved in playing one's chosen instrument—the fingers, the breath, the facial muscles, the neck, the back. Certain movements must be repeated so often that they can be performed on the instrument effortlessly, even in unusual positions.

This is not to suggest that the cognitive and emotional aspects of music training in any way play a secondary role. Ideally, practice should produce not only technical mastery of a piece but also insight into the music's structure and content, both of which are discussed during instruction.

## Interpretation

The discussion component of musical education usually involves questions of interpretation. Teacher and student may engage in exchanges, as between equals, regarding a given piece's structure, tone, or affect. At this point (and throughout any student's musical education), the student is no longer simply learning through imitation, but is expressing himself or herself creatively. The final aim is the development of the sudent's own musical personality.

## Teacher—Student

Most instrument teachers have several students who come to share his or her musical perspectives and approach to playing. The resulting music (either in performance or in composition) tends to be characterized by certain common principles of interpretation and stylistic idiosyncrasies, sometimes for generations. We then come to speak of a teacher and his or her protegés, or school, or of a national school, characterized by a unified aesthetic view. In piano music, for example, we may hear of the "school" of Franz Liszt, whose playing technique became the

foundation of European piano teaching within a few generations.

## Music competitions

Public performance of music is part and parcel of our musical education system. In both amateur and professional recitals, competitive thinking often drives musical pursuit. The music competition is not simply a matter of interpretation and polish, but involves an evaluation that is not intrinsic to the music itself: It may involve personal as well as national tastes and biases. Still, any musician who wants to pursue a solo career must achieve success at an international competition.

**53** The composition "Islamej" by Mili Balakirew. Even for a piano student of extremely high technical ability, the difficulties of this piece place it beyond the reach of all but a few really excellent pianists.

**Hornbostel and Sachs**

"The work of classification is in general somewhat suspect. Whatever is supposed to be organized and systemized came into existence unsystematically, and grew and changed with-out taking consideration of a comprehensible scheme." So begins *The Organization of Music Instruments* by Erich Moritz von Hornbostel (**54**) and Curt Sachs (**55**), revealing the authors' clear awareness of the hazards of attempting to impose a static form of organization on all the instruments of the world. Such a system must rest on an organizing principle that is at once simple, consistent, and inclusive. On the other hand, it must be sufficiently flexible to accommodate precisely the dynamism and changeability of musical instruments throughout the course of their historical development.

In the approach of their colleague Mahillon, Hornbostel and Sachs found the underlying principles so well suited for their system that they adopted them with few changes. The common basis is the physical process of producing a tone by causing air to vibrate.

Hornbostel and Sachs's reflections and thought processes at first glance appear strictly theoretical and academic—prompted, so it seems, by some personal need for a system and order. The practical utility of their work, however, becomes evident when one visits a museum or repository of musical instruments where the names Mahillon, Horn-bostel, and Sachs are unknown. In

**54**  Erich Moritz von Hornbostel (1877–1935), an Austrian scholar, was one of the founders of comparative musicology. His standard classification of musical instruments (produced in collaboration with Curt Sachs) is his most important contribution to this scientific discipline.

such places, the lack of universal anchors creates confusion in particular when folk, or ethnological, labels are used as the organizing principle. For example, the jew's harp (originally, jaw's harp), sometimes called the guimbard or the mouth drum (from the German, "Maultrommel"), is in fact neither a harp nor a drum but an instrument with a vibrating metal tongue. To categorize it according to any of its common names would most likely be quite misleading.

In 1914, Hornbostel and Sachs ended this capricious and arbitrary system of grouping entirely different types and forms of instruments. In their *Standard Classification of Musical Instruments*, they arranged instruments more rationally. Amended today to include instruments that produce sound electrically or electronically, this landmark work is still used for both scientific and practical purposes.

55  Curt Sachs (1881 – 1959), together with Erich Moritz von Hornbostel, developed the standard classification for musical instruments. Born in Berlin, Sachs was deprived of his academic positions by the Nazis in 1933 and lived in the United States from 1937 until his death. The science of musical instruments remained his chief area of interest within the field of ethnomusicology.

## The system in practice

Guiding the work of Hornbostel and Sachs is a uniform principle of organization based on natural physical attributes. The consistency this approach allows prevents major errors in the organization of the instruments, though in itself, it does not go beyond dividing instruments into four groups according to the origin of the sound: vibrations produced by the instrument itself ("self-sounding"), by a skin or membrane ("skin-sounding"), by strings ("string-sounding"), or by movement of air ("air-sounding"). Hornbostel and Sachs painstakingly elaborated characteristics whose presence or absence would define the instrument more precisely. A closer look at these criteria reveals two primary elements of differentiation:

**56** Bells are found all around the world. For the study of musical instruments, the question of how they produce their sound is of great significance. As a rule, a free-swinging tongue or clapper hangs inside the bell, but one can also produce the tone by striking a mallet against the bell from the outside.

**57** The technical instrumental differences that distinguish a harp from other string instruments are obvious.

1. The naming of the individual parts of an instrument and how these contribute to the production of sound;
2. How the player produces the tone.

The importance of an instrument's various components is directly related to their acoustical function. Thus, the tongue of a bell is not as critical as it might seem at first glance because a bell can produce a sound by being struck by another object (**56**). For string instruments—whether a violin, a zither, or a washtub bass—on the other hand, the strings are essential; whether they are drawn over a soundbox (as in the violin) or not (as in the harp, or the washtub bass) is not critical for the production of a tone, and is therefore only a secondary characteristic. The system, thus, is based on a series of primary and secondary distinctions that arise rather strictly from their function.

As a rule, Hornbostel and Sachs describe the production of musical sound in terms that the layperson can understand: Parts of the instruments are plucked, scraped, shaken, struck (upon or against one another), blown, rubbed, or otherwise acted upon. The finer technical aspects of varying the tones

or the possibility for virtuoso development are not taken into account here. Even if these musicologists do use lay terms to describe the production of tone, they borrow the rest of their terminology, as is traditional in certain scientific fields, from Greek. Hence, the formal categories: instruments that produce tones of themselves are called idiophones, instruments with vellum and stretched skins are called membranophones, string instruments are called chordaphones, and wind instruments are called aerophones.

## Rattles, gongs, and castanets

It is easy enough to understand that an idiophone is something that is shaken or struck or hit against another object or itself. To picture a "plucked polyheteroglottal idiophone," however, requires either fluency in Greek or a certain familiarity with the terminology—not unlike the degree of familiarity one needs

58 Castanet player Lucero Tena.

to read the ingredients and indications on an over-the-counter cold remedy. Once one is fairly familiar with such specialized terminology, it becomes clear that the African zansa or mbira (37), which is known in ethnic music and collectible shops and catalogs as a thumb piano, answers this description because the several loosely fastened tongues or tabs make a sound when they are plucked. A jew's harp, with only a single flexible metal tongue, may be described as a "plucked monoheteroglottal idiophone."

## Drumskins and drumbeats

The tremendous variety of drum instruments from around the world posed no particular problem for the Hornbostel and Sachs typology; their lack of structural characteristics, however, did complicate the process of

59 Drums from the Indian subcontinent.

59 Drums from the Indian subcontinent.

distinguishing among them all. Hornbostel and Sachs addressed this complication by enumerating and describing how the membrane is fastened to the rest of the instrument. To characterize a drum more precisely, they turn to a secondary characteristic—specifically, the form of the resonator, or body, of the drum. Thus, there are barrel drums, kettle drums, tubular drums, and so on. The problems with this kind of classification were not lost on Hornbostel and Sachs: For example, should they distinguish between a drum with a frame (such as a tamborine) and a tubular drum with a cylindrical shape (such as a snare drum) by the height of the frame or the cylinder? It is easy to see that the boundaries must remain very fluid.

## Strings in harmony

"One or more strings are stretched between two fixed points." In this terse description, Hornbostel and Sachs identify the defining characteristic of the chordaphones. It is of no consequence, for

60 The zither is one of the so-called simple chordaphones.

61 Early models of the grand piano, such as this early 19th-century instrument, had a straight row of strings. Pianos are classified as a simple chordophone.

their system, whether the fixed points are found on a straight or a bowed neck, or on a board, a shell-shaped body, or a frame.

The presence or absence of a sound box does not alter the instrument's essence: although a sound box completely changes the character of the tone, it has no effect on the manner (for typological purposes, of course) in which that tone is produced.

If, however, a resonator is so organically bound with the surface or body to which the strings are attached that it cannot be removed without destroying both it-self and the terminal point of the strings, then Hornbos-tel and Sachs designate the instrument a *compos-ite chordaphone*. Thus, the zither (**60**) and the pia-no (**61**) are simple chorda-

62 The guitar is a composite chordaphone.

phones because the resonator can be removed without destroying the function of the instrument. Violins and guitars (**62**), on the other hand, are composite chordaphones because it is not possible to remove the sound box without essentially destroying the instrument (by making it incapable of producing the sound it was designed to produce). For the simple chordaphone, Hornbostel and Sachs adopt the term *zither*; for composite instruments, the term *lute*—both rather unfortunate choices that generate confusion because the zither and the lute are also specific instruments.

**63** Flutes can be either transverse or straight. This picture by Johann Kupezky shows a man playing a transverse flute; the name is derived from how the instrument is held.

### Blowing hot air?

Hornbostel and Sachs's distinction between "open" aerophones and true wind instruments pinpoints an aspect of such instruments that is not always immediately apparent. By open or free aerophones, they mean instruments that cause the air to vibrate but that do not impede or control the air movement; examples might be a whip or a blade of grass, when you hold it between your fingers and blow against it.

This classification becomes problematic when the tongued pipes of a church organ are counted among the open or free aerophones simply because they cause air to vibrate. Following the same reasoning, one could classify the pipes as idiophones on the basis of the

**64** Flute made of animal bone.

movement of their elastic tongues. At the same time one could argue that the true wind instruments—including flutes, clarinets, and oboes according to Hornbostel and Sachs—are also idiophones because the air is set in motion by a single (in the clarinet) or a double (in the oboe) reed. In the entire family of flutes—straight, cross, German, transverse, with or without fingerholes—a column of air is pushed by the air from the player's lips through a fully stationary channel; the column of air is thus directly made to vibrate. While this process is truly aerophonic, it would be splitting hairs to insist on counting the clarinet and oboe as idiophones.

On the whole, this system proves useful for examining instruments in their social environment in spite of certain small inconsistencies introduced by an occasional misplaced emphasis on one or another aspect of the instruments. Idiophones and membranophones are, for example, characterized by the primary form of their tone production, which is, in theory, a very reasonable approach. In contrast, chordaphones are defined as either simple or composite according to structural elements, and aerophones are defined through a mixture of functional and constructive details according to the presence or absence of restraints affecting the movement of air.

**65**  Mouthpieces of various wind instruments (top to bottom): a clarinet, an oboe, and a recorder.

**66**  This flute player is playing a straight flute, or recorder. Its German name Blockflöte comes from the wooden block in the interior of the instrument.

### With white and black keys

We hear a great deal of recorded music in our daily lives—from our radios, televisions, personal stereos (Walkmen and portable CD players), in the supermarket, in elevators, waiting on hold on the telephone—but only rarely do we think of how that music is made. As listeners, we tend to hear music as a product, stored on electronic media and reproduced electronically. We are just as unclear about the technical requirements of the telecasts that flicker daily and continuously in most of our homes. Those who play live music or hear it performed without electronic means may better appreciate that music making itself is a technical process (**67**). When we attend a concert—whether it is the Boston Symphony or the Boston Pops, in a concert hall or a coffee-house, in a church or a museum or at a back-yard barbecue, on a streetcorner in midtown Manhattan or in an underground station in London—we have an experience that is unlike hearing recorded music, and as such, may prompt a number of peculiar impressions and questions having to do with the purely musical.

A world-class pianist in recital does not play on a spinet with its tone dampened so as not to disturb the neighbors. He or she plays on a large grand piano designed for the concert hall,

**67** The playing console of a modern organ. Large instruments have up to four, sometimes even five manuals (keyboards).

on an instrument that vastly outperforms the home piano in fullness of tone. Likewise, the concert organist pulling out all the stops is showing off not only the quality of the instrument but also his or her own skill and/or voice. In summer concert series at Tanglewood or Lyndhurst, in stately homes and art museums, in concerts with a baroque repertoire, even ensembles using modern instruments are likely to retain the obligato keyboard part which is often improvised along with the instrumental parts. Among street musicians, many of whom piece together an accompaniment from a few meager guitar chords, one may still hear the neglected accordion (68) ringing out with a sharp tone through the tumult of voices. Otherwise, one must look for this instrument in wedding bands playing polkas, waltzes, and tangos, and at obscure local fairs and contests.

These are the keyboards. Though they fit into different slots in a Hornbostel and Sachs schema, they all share the feature of the black and white keys which unites them in the minds of most people.

While this popular overarching category conveniently known as keyboard instruments may defy musicologists' classifications, it nonetheless encompasses a wide variety of instruments, many of which share a certain cultural and social history and evolution. There are, in short, connections between the organ and the harpsichord, and the piano (whose history has been less restricted to specific geo-

**68** The accordion is an aerophone; it may be played by pressing buttons (left) or a keyboard (above).

**69** The hurdy-gurdy also has a keyboard mechanism. The player's left hand presses keys to depress the strings and thus change the pitch. The player's right hand turns a crank, which operates a wheel that acts as a circular bow, setting the string vibrating.

Keyboard Instruments

**70** A piano is an outspoken solo instrument. A contemporary caricature of composer and pianist Camille Saint-Saëns (1835–1925).

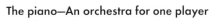

graphic areas and musical styles) and the accordion, with its somewhat narrower popular social history.

**71** Pianos may be technologically altered so that they can play automatically and make all sorts of "unpianistic" sounds.

### The piano—An orchestra for one player

Virtually no other instrument used in western music can challenge the position held by the piano in the consciousness of musicians and music lovers. In all branches of music, in all styles and directions, from classical music, where it is so often heard solo, to jazz and most forms of pop music (including synthesized), the piano is indispensable. Perhaps the only western music tradition that is not dominated by the piano is, for obvious reasons, the folk music tradition, which grew out of a heritage of strolling and traveling, for which the piano was clearly ill-suited.

One aspect of the piano's versatility is that it allows the musician to play many parts at once, and therefore spans the entire pitch ranges of many other instruments. Meanwhile, its ingenious mechanics can give a degree of flexibility and nuance to individual tones otherwise available only from some string and wind instruments.

72 A hammered dulcimer.

## A wooden zither with a striking mechanism

The history of keyboard instruments in general, and of pianos in particular, usually begins with an ancient non-European cittern (a precursor to the zither); this is followed by a medieval psaltery, and then, finally, by a clavichord. Of course, most texts will not suggest that the cittern is a precursor of the piano, but they are likely to point out connections among the basic details of construction. Parallel ordered strings are stretched tightly over two bridges and can thus vibrate together. As a rule, a cittern was played with the hands while a psaltery was played either with the fingers or with a plectrum. The psaltery has also been adapted to be played with small hammers or mallets, as in the hammered dulcimer

73 A *Hammerklavier* (early piano) from the time of Ludwig van Beethoven.

common to Appalachia (72) and popular among certain Celtic music traditions.

The clavichord is an early stringed keyboard instrument found in use from the 15th century. Attached to each key is a lever mechanism that presses a small brass blade called a tangent until it strikes the string to produce a soft tone that can be modulated by different finger techniques to alter the tone, create a swelling effect, or even to produce a vibrato. The harpsichord also uses a key mechanism, but it uses a quill plectrum to pluck the string (74). The harpsichord produces a comparatively stiff and inflexible tone. Both instruments were popular throughout Europe through the end of the 18th century.

## Cristofori, Silbermann, Erard

The 17th-century Italian keyboard instrument maker Bartolomeo Cristofori sought to combine the modulation capabilities of the clavichord with the louder volume of a harpsichord. Around 1700, he experimented with a rebounding hammer mechanism to replace the plectrum used in a harpsichord. This would allow the hammer to meet the string at varying speeds. In other

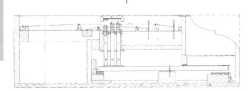

74  Schematic of a harpsichord mechanism.

75  The psaltery, plucked here by an angel with a quill, is a precursor to the harpsichord. The harpsichord has retained this wing-shaped form. Pianos, however, were soon built in varied shapes.

words, the depressing of the key, the touch, would directly determine the volume, tonal character, and duration of the pitch. Cristofori's mechanics were based on a princi-

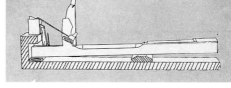

76 Metal tongue escapement mechanism.

ple whereby a mechanical connection between key and hammer allowed considerable modulation of volume (**76**). The action consists of a pivoted lever set in motion by a key. As the lever rises to strike the string, an under-damping mechanism is lowered to allow

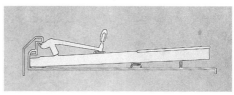

77 Prell mechanism.

the string to vibrate after the leather-covered hammer springs back. Cristofori called this instrument an "arpicembalo che fá il piano e il forte," which means a "harpsichord with loud and soft" (i.e., variations in dynamics). In the following decades, the increasingly popular instrument be-

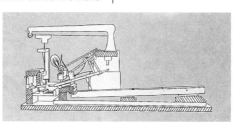

78 Metal tongue escapement mechanism.

came known as either the fortepiano or the pianoforte. Today, three pianos built by Cristofori survive; the oldest, dated 1720, is in New York.

The Silbermanns were a German family of organ builders and instrument makers. Gottfried Silbermann, a contemporary of Cristofori, also constructed an instrument that used a hammer mechanism, but his dispensed with Cristofori's lever mechanism and allowed the hammer to strike the string directly when the key was depressed. Silbermann's process became known as the Prell mechanism, but these pianos (**77**) did not prevail because their fixed mechanism limited volume and created too heavy an action.

The French instrument builder Sébastien Erard in Paris based the mechanism for his grand piano on Cristofori's design, which he developed further and enriched with a revolutionary invention (**78**). In Erard's instrument, if the hammer hits the string quickly, the escapement releases so that it hits the string with its own momentum. When it falls back, it returns to the starting position, but not until the player completely re-

**79** The external form of the grand piano has not changed since the 19th century.

leases the key. Erard developed a complicated "feather" mechanism that allowed the release of the hammer when the key was only halfway back up. This allowed for much faster repetition of notes.

**80** Steel frame of a grand piano.

## Ever bigger, ever louder

With the development of the mechanism in grand and upright pianos, the external form of the instruments also evolved. While their register expanded, the desire to produce a bigger sound that could reach the back rows in concert halls called for a fundamental structural change (**79**). The earliest pianos were built entirely from wood, but in the late 18th century an iron frame was added to stabilize the soundboard (**80**). This allowed more resilient materials to be used for the strings, which could be thicker and produce a more ringing tone. Strings were made of steel, with the large bass strings wrapped in copper. For the higher notes, the hammer strikes three identical strings simultaneously which sound together. The leather that covered the hammer was replaced by felt, and these developments produced what we think of as the piano's sound today. With its technical evolution essentially complete, nothing limited the development of piano virtuosity, for which demand would increase.

### Electric piano and digital piano

There are two kinds of pianos that use electronic components. Pianos in which the primary sound is produced electronically by means of a tone generator or other electronic source are synthesizers, while electric pianos (**81**), which might more accurately be described as electromechanical, generate sound by striking metal tines (as in the Fender and Wurlitzer electric keyboards) or strings (as in some Yamaha electric pianos), using electrical pickups, as in electric guitars, to amplify the sound.

**81** An electric piano looks very much like an acoustic spinet.

The player piano offers a different sort of variation on the mechanical action of the conventional piano. It might rightly be called a reproducing piano in which some kind of stored information sets in motion the action of a regular acoustic piano. The earliest player pianos were developed at the turn of the century; information (what we would today call data) that would direct the mechanical action of an otherwise ordinary (and functional as a manual) piano was recorded on a perforated paper roll. The mechanism was originally powered by pumping foot pedals, and later by electricity. There is a "high-tech" counterpart to the player piano in which the music roll is replaced by a magnetic (computer) diskette, though in the grand scheme of available music-making media today, this kind of digital piano is not common, nor is it likely to be.

### Pianos for the living room, the barroom, and the concert hall

There is no fundamental mechanical difference between an "ordinary" piano and a concert grand if one is unable to perceive the differences in sound. The differences are in fact purely a matter of acoustics (occasionally one of aesthetics as well). Listen to an immature piano student struggling through Beethoven's "Feuille d'Album," a bagatelle in A minor inscribed "Für Elise." Or a jazzman playing Dixieland music with a band in an after-hours dive. Then listen to an accomplished conservatory student or a successful concert pianist sitting at a grand piano in a recital hall. Is it fair to associate the humble or unpretentious performance, the popular or bohemian or counterculture style, with the upright piano? Is it accurate to associate the concert grand with artistic perfection and "high culture"? The fact is that the piano is a universally popular instrument that serves different functions in different social circles, and our assumptions about what it signifies in any one context may not be relevant.

In a modest student apartment, a grand piano is a sure sign of a serious pianist in residence. In a Central Park West apartment or a Beverly Hills living room, it may be nothing more than a sign of wealth and a status symbol on which to arrange family photographs. And, while classical concert pianists invariably perform on high-quality grand pianos, so do Elton John and Billy Joel and other pop/rock keyboard players.

**82** Carl Philipp Emanuel Bach (1714-88) was one of the first composers who wrote music expressly for the piano.

**83** In the works of Ludwig van Beethoven (1750-1827), the thread of piano music weaves everywhere. In all his creative periods, he wrote piano music.

## Piano music

With its great range and its versatility, the piano lends itself to almost any music, and so has attracted countless composers and musicians.

The first compositions written explicitly for the piano, and not originally or simultaneously written for the other stringed keyboard instru-

ments, the harpsichord and clavichord, were produced in the mid-18th century. In *On the True Art of Playing the Piano*, Carl Philipp Emanuel Bach (1714–88, **82**), explicated the theoretical underpinnings of his own piano compositions.

In the ensuing decades, nearly every composer wrote for the piano. The piano works of Ludwig van Beethoven (**83**) demanded considerably greater virtuosity of the pianist than did either of his predecessors, Joseph Haydn (1732–1809) and Wolfgang Amadeus Mozart (1756–91). Just a few decades after Beethoven wrote, piano music was infused with the invention and innovations of Frédéric Chopin (1810–49) and Franz Liszt (1811–86, **84**), both of whom were known as virtuoso players themselves, the latter with a following to rival today's superstars. In 20th-century art music, Maurice Ravel (1875–1937), Claude Debussy (1862–1918), and Béla Bartòk (1881–1945, **85**) have composed especially impressive works for the piano.

**84** A caricature of Franz Liszt, who set a standard for technical virtuosity in piano playing.

**85** In his piano music, Béla Bartòk incorporated many elements of Hungarian folk music.

**86** The piano is a principal instrument in jazz. Keith Jarrett is one of the most famous contemporary jazz pianists.

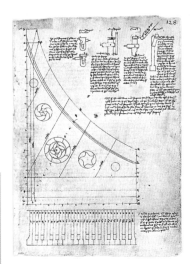

**87** The oldest known harpsichord blueprint. Many historically conscious harpsichord makers today use old plans.

The piano repertoire from the mid-18th century until today includes both expansive, strictly organized forms like the sonata, the concerto, and cycles of variations, and smaller forms like dances, ballads, fantasias, and rhapsodies.

In jazz, the piano may assume both the supporting part of filling in the harmony and improvising a melody over its own scaffolding (**86**), while the piano bar (complete with a shell for holding a tip bowl and customers' cocktails) serves up a corny combination of song leading, sentiment, and occasionally a reserve of skill. Pop music and pop culture offer many niches for the piano and the pianist. Rock and roll artists heavily influenced by blues and boogie-woogie, such as Jerry Lee Lewis and Little Richard, feature their piano playing, while some famous rock musicians, such as Elton John come to rock from a classical background, opting for the piano and keyboards over the more common lead guitar.

## The harpsichord

The "invention" of the pianoforte by Cristofori in the early 18th century gradually overshadowed the harpsichord, even as it adapted its original hammer mechanism. Still, the harpsichord maintains a secure place in musical history and attracts its own special following.

The harpsichord, as already suggested, can trace its evolution back to the medieval

**88** A harpsichord jack to which the quill plectrum is attached.

psaltery. The psaltery, an instrument in the zither family with a wooden sound box with rows of strings stretched between metal pins, could be struck with mallets or plucked with a plectrum, which was the more common method of playing the medieval instruments. In time, the sound box was enlarged and the plucking process mechanized and augmented with a keyboard. Some additional components were added and the accumulated modifications eventually produced what we know as the harpsichord. For this reason, there is no one to name as the instrument's inventor (**87**). It emerged in this form sometime around 1400; in a 1440 treatise, the Dutch theorist Henri Arnault de Zwolle describes the "clavisimbalum"—that is, a psaltery with keys. The construction of the harpsichord's plucking mechanism has essentially remained the same since the instrument's earliest appearance. It consists of a simple lever, the key, which, when depressed, raises a small rod, called the spindle or jack (**88**). The jack is tipped by a small quill or plectrum, originally made of bird feather but now of plastic. This quill plucks the string, but an escapement mechanism makes sure that it does not repluck it when the key is released. The harpsichord's sound is static and rather inflexible because the rapidity and strength with which the key is struck does not influence its tone, as it does on the piano. Harpsichordists remedy

89
Most harpsichords have one or two manuals. A three-manual instrument was a status symbol in the baroque period.

90 Harpsichord soundboards were often decoratively painted, as in this instrument. Such ornamentation increases the instrument's value as a status symbol; it has little effect on the sound.

Keyboard Instruments

**91, 92** The wing-form harpsichords were to some extent the standard, though some instruments were more rectangular, or even polygonal in shape. The virginal (from the Latin *virga*, spindle) was generally rectangular, the spinet (from Latin *spina*, thorn, quill) usually had many corners.

these "deficiencies" through a refined musical technique, using controlled tempo changes, holding and repeating certain keys, and other such maneuvers.

The strings of a harpsichord are stretched tightly in a longitudinal direction over an enclosed soundboard. At the keyboard end, the string is wound around a tuning pin that can be tightened or loosened to correct the pitch; at the other end, the string is fixed to a metal hitchpin. Depending on the string's material and the place at which the string is plucked, the instrument can produce a plethora of tonal differences, making each harpsichord a unique instrument. Each harpsichord may have several sets of strings that can be used individually or in different combinations. Each set of strings with the same tonal character over the entire range of an instrument is called a register. Registers are labeled with a number according to an old system that refers to organ pipes. For example, the register that sounds the fundamental pitches throughout the instrument's range are called 8-foot registers, because 8 feet is the standard length of the lowest pipe of concert pitch in organ building. The register that sounds an octave higher than the 8 foot throughout the range of the instrument is labeled 4 foot, the register that sounds an octave lower 16 foot, and so on. The combination of several registers, such as two 8 foot and a 4 foot, yields a silvery, sometimes a rustling sound, which was enjoyed in the baroque period as expressive of festivity and pomp.

In order to vary the timbre even more, harpsichord makers began to build instruments with more than one keyboard. The musician could play two different registers or combinations simultaneously—the melody with one tonal color and the

93 A clavichord of Hieronymus Albrecht Hass, Hamburg, 1728.

accompaniment with another. Also, technical changes of the different registers widened the tonal possibilities. The Lautenwerk had a wooden molding with small felt blocks that pressed against the string, softening the tone to make it sound more like a lute.

Harpsichords, like organs (see p. 60), owe their versatility to certain built-in technical elements such as variations in the sounds of each instrument's registers.

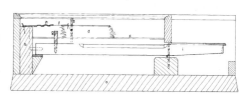

94 Schematic of the clavichord mechanism.

However, unlike the piano or the clavichord, the individual player's technique in depressing the key has no effect on the quality of the tone or the volume of the sound.

## The clavichord

"Whoever it was," wrote Sebastian Virdung in 1511 in *Musica getutscht,* "that discovered or imagined it ... and therefore baptized the clavichord and gave it its name, I know not." It is

95 A clavichord key with its tangent.

hardly surprising that by the beginning of the 16th century no one could remember who invented the clavichord (the name, on the other hand, is self-explanatory: *clavis* = key and *chorda* = string). It takes no great genius to furnish a stringed soundboard with keys attached to a brass pin that taps a string. The clavichord is nothing if not a model of simplicity of design underlying an unusual musical effect, which, according to contemporary opinion of the subsequent 250 years, was not to be outdone.

The small metal pin, called a tangent (from the Latin *tangere*, to touch), is less than half an inch high and fans out slightly at the top; it touches the string when the key is depressed. This touching, which is less a striking motion than a gentle pressing of the key, produces a very soft tone that can only be perceived by careful listening (**95**). The clavichord's dynamic range extends from approximately mezzo forte (medium loud) at its upper end down to pianississississimo (very very very soft), which is nearly inaudible. Beyond this dynamic range, the tone, which takes some getting used to, proves unusually variable. A clavichord player can actually produce a "vibrato" or "tremolo"—after depressing the key, while the string is sounding, the player applies a bit more pressure using a lateral motion of the finger; this produces a slight oscillation in pitch.

Two kinds of clavichords are distinguished according to the construction of the key mechanism. Earlier instruments did not have an individual string to correspond to each different pitch. Instead, several keys' tangents struck a single string at different places, thereby producing different pitches; this is known as a "fretted" clavichord (**96**). If each string is in fact struck by only one tangent, the clavichord is "unfretted." The need for unfretted mechanisms became more urgent with the growing complexity of harmony in 17th- and

**96** A fretted clavichord.

18th-century music; such harmonic arrangements included chords that were simply not possible on the fretted instruments because their notes lay on the same string. Clavichords were practical and inexpensive to make. Typical instruments ranged from slightly over 3 feet wide, 14 inches deep, to 5 feet wide and 18 inches deep. Until the early classical period when they were finally displaced, along with the harpsichord, by the piano, they tended to be used as second or practice instruments in musical households.

97  Johann Sebastian Bach (1685–1750).

### Late blooming

Beside its function as a practice instrument, the clavichord had a particular appeal for composers of the so-called "sensitive style" around the mid-18th century because the instrument seemed peculiarly suited to express all the emotions and moods called forth by the music. With emotional and, as it were, psychical inspiration an esteemed quality in music at the time, people were supposedly often moved to tears by the music of the clavichord.

### Clavichord and harpsichord music

Carl Philipp Emanuel Bach (**82**) composed clavichord music that was particularly suited to the "arousal of the feelings" so in vogue in his day. He actually indicated exactly which of his compositions were to be played on the clavichord, the harpsichord, or piano. Earlier composers did not often consider these distinctions necessary. The works of his father, Johann Sebastian Bach (**97**), if not written explicitly for a harpsichord with two manuals (keyboards) or for the organ, can be played as written on the clavichord, which in his famous *Well-Tempered Clavier* was tacitly assumed. Harpsichord music, which does not appear absolutely suitable also for the clavichord, reached its peak with the French composers François Couperin (**98**), his uncle Louis Couperin, Jac-

98  François Couperin (1668–1733).

99  Domenico Scarlatti (1685–1757).

ques Champion de Chambonnières, and others. Their music consisted mainly of highly stylized miniatures assembled into suites. Suites based on dance forms also comprised the bulk of the harpsichord music by German and English composers. In Italy and Spain, on the other hand, Domenico Scarlatti (99) left behind a body of work overwhelmingly dominated by harpsichord sonatas.

The early sonatas of Haydn and Mozart were written for either the harpsichord or the clavichord. Near the end of the 18th century, the tradition of harpsichord and clavichord came to an abrupt, and total, halt. The early 20th century, however, brought renewed interest in the harpsichord, for which some composers such as Manuel de Falla and Francis Poulenc wrote concertos. Composers today continue to write for the harpsichord, such as György Ligeti, whose 1968 *Continuum* breathed new life into contemporary harpsichord music.

## The organ

Even people who have no interest in music, and still less in musical instruments, know the organ (100), if for no other reason than that it is the instrument of church music. The organ is a technically, mechanically, and visually intricate, highly crafted instrument that is commonly associated with baroque pageantry. In fact, it was during the baroque period that the organ's long evolution reached a peak, marked by its greatest blossom-

100 Organs from the baroque era are elaborately and expensively decorated.

ing and launching into the instrument's increasing mechanization. In the expansion and growing complexity of its design, which integrated many individual elements into a single whole, the organ served as a metaphor for the divine order, as expounded by philosophers and theologians of this world and the next. There were also purely musical reasons driving the changes in the organ's mechanisms and sound—changes which were to turn the organ into the large instrument we know.

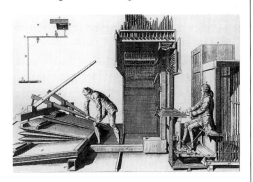

101  Building plan of an organ. A "calcant" worked the bellows to supply the organ pipes with air. Nearly all present-day organs are equipped with electric blowers.

### Keys, air, and pipes

Only a fraction of the individual parts of the organ that produce and regulate its sound are visible to the viewer. Its most striking features are its rows of pipes, arranged by length, only one series of which is visible; its two (or more) keyboards, stacked on top of one another, which are played with the hands; and another keyboard of pedals underneath the console, which is played with the feet. The view inside an organ confirms the presumption that it is a supremely complicated machine—an apparent tangle of bars, wires, pipes, and wooden cases (101).

### The "box of whistles"

A bellows is filled with air, which is held under constant pressure. This air passes over a hinged valve, which is opened by pressing a key in the

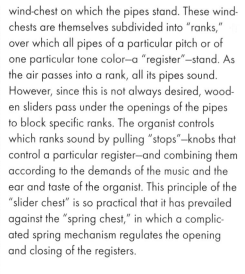

wind-chest on which the pipes stand. These wind-chests are themselves subdivided into "ranks," over which all pipes of a particular pitch or of one particular tone color—a "register"—stand. As the air passes into a rank, all its pipes sound. However, since this is not always desired, wooden sliders pass under the openings of the pipes to block specific ranks. The organist controls which ranks sound by pulling "stops"—knobs that control a particular register—and combining them according to the demands of the music and the ear and taste of the organist. This principle of the "slider chest" is so practical that it has prevailed against the "spring chest," in which a complicated spring mechanism regulates the opening and closing of the registers.

### Bars and wires

The keys and the valve on the underside of the wind-chest are connected via the bars and the molding system, which are the first thing one sees upon looking inside an organ. These cause the traction that the organist feels when depressing the key directly, as the air streams into the wind-chest. Besides organs with these mechanical "tracker actions," there are instruments in which the valve is opened by an electric mechanism in which an electric circuit runs from the manual keyboards and the pedal keyboards into the wind and pipeworks.

Electric ventilators, which provide the bellows with air, are ubiquitous on modern organs, and even on reproductions of historic organs. Before electric power was available, the bellows were pumped by old-fashioned muscle power, supplied by a person called a "calcant." A few really serious baroque reproduction organs still have hand- or foot-pumped bellows. Some organ restorers now fix up the old manual bellows but also install a motor so that either method can be used.

102  This small portable organ is called a Bible Regal

## Flue stops and reed stops

The organ's different registers provide a great variety of different tonal colors, determined in part by the materials used to make the pipes (wood or metal), and in part by their design. As in all aerophones, in the organ pipe, a column of air is set vibrating. This happens in two ways: Like a whistle, the airstream meets with an edge (lip) and is divided, or a metal tongue (reed) conducts its own oscillation to the surrounding air. These two completely different tone properties—the purer sounding flue registers and the sharper sounding reed registers—determine the tonal character of an organ. Structural changes, such as the closing of a pipe at its upper end, produce further variation and enrich the sound. These covered pipes sound an octave lower than the open pipe of equal length. The sound of an organ is further characterized by groups of different pipes that sound intervals of a fifth or an octave above the basic pitch; these are called

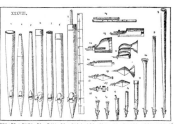

103 Diagram of different organ pipes from the *Syntagma musicum* by Michael Praetorius.

Keyboard Instruments

104 Organ reed pipes. The small metal rods regulate the tuning of the individual pipes.

mixtures and they accentuate certain overtones of the tonal spectrum. It is in fact difficult to render the full complexity of the organ in so little space. A guided tour through an actual organ would help. Occasionally nicknamed the "Queen of Instruments," the organ offers the musician a challenge well beyond the distinction conferred by this popular sobriquet. For one thing, its technical complexity puts more distance between the performer and the sound: Besides having to pull stops and stomp their feet on the pedals while tickling the ivories, the organist often must persist in the face of a delay between the time he or she plays the notes and the time they sound. The organist has to perform the music before hearing it and continue to play out of synch with the sound—a much more cerebral exercise than required by other, more immediate, less royal instruments.

## Sacral function

The organ has a longstanding tradition in the church and in sacred music. In Christian worship services (and Jewish services insofar as they allow any accompaniment), it is generally the only musical instrument, except on special occasions that may include instrumental ensembles. The organ also plays a role in concerts of religious music from the baroque period (17th–18th centuries), such as performances of Handel's *Messiah* or Bach's *St. Matthew Passion*. For such works, the organist plays only the "basso continuo," an elaboration of the harmony over the composer's bass line. A relatively small organ with only a few registers, the positive, is used in the orchestra for these pieces. Late romantic composers (19th century) and modern composers have also written symphonic works with organ parts, as well as bravura solo organ pieces. These are usually played on large concert hall organs and may or may not have any religious connotation.

**105** Jan Pieterszoon Sweelinck (1562–1621).

## Organ music

From the 17th century on, music for the organ and other keyboard instruments, which in early music can be clearly divided between the sacred and the secular, assumed a more technical, instrument-specific dimension. The expansion of the pedalboard, especially on north German organs, allowed the organist to play a separate voice and was used by composers extensively to create an independent organ music. J.S. Bach's compositions for organ, which call upon the traditions of northern and southern Germany as well as of Italy, are generally thought of as the pinnacle of the repertoire. In the Netherlands and in north Germany, organ music assumed particular importance through composers such as Jan Pieterszoon Sweelinck (**105**) and Dietrich Buxtehude (1632–1707). The most important Italian composer of organ music is Girolamo Frescobaldi (ca. 1583–1643).

**106**  The playing console of the organ in Arnstadt, Germany. Johann Sebastian Bach played on this instrument.

Pieces in which church melodies were artfully elaborated (such as chorale preludes), and pieces written to show off the tonal possibilities of the organ and virtuosity of the player (such as toccatas), along with the the severe contrapuntal forms of the fugue and the ricercar, form the kernel of the baroque organ repertoire.

In the second half of the 19th century, organ music experienced a new peak, particularly in France where it grew to symphonic dimensions. Most notable are the compositions of César Franck (1822–90) and Camille Saint-Saëns. Max Reger (**107**) brought powerful compositions and especially rich harmony to the German organ music of his time. The most important 20th-century organ composer is the Frenchman Olivier Mes-

**107**  Max Reger (1873–1916).

siaen (1908–92), whose music combines complex structure with an unusual tonal language (he claims to have been especially influenced by natural sounds, such as bird song).

## Hammond Organ to Soundmachine

Today, the designation "keyboards" is less likely to draw to mind ornate baroque instruments giving voice to two or three-part inventions than to summon the image of the pop musician hammering away at an array of electronic keyboards producing a nearly symphonic array of synthesized and/or electric sound. By the 1930s musicians were experimenting with electronic tone generation, and the vision emerged of a technology that offers endless possibilities for assembling and reassembling sounds and for manufacturing new sounds synthetically. The charm of keyboard playing increases as its complicated technology becomes less complicated for the user. With the push of a button, an electronic keyboard can issue a multitude of sounds of different instruments, from a trumpet or a cello to a helicopter or a UFO. The traditional instrument sounds are more or less authentic, depending on the quality of the keyboard. While an inexpensive, toylike, three-octave mini-keyboard may only hint at real sound quality, more technically advanced (and more expensive) keyboards do offer correspondingly better-quality sounds. The sounds themselves are stored electronically on the "soundcard," and prepared so that the player can retrieve them individually or as small musical sequences. While these keyboards may not compete with a Steinway concert grand, they are accessible for the less affluent and might, perhaps, best be seen as a new sort of instrument that does not need to compete with traditional instruments, but serves its own purposes.

**108**  The Hammond organ was one of the first instruments with electronic tone generation available to the general public. Its sound was especially popular in the 1970s.

**109**  The kind of keyboard used with a music computer.

**110** Synthesizer keyboard. Producing and manipulating sounds artfully can be a thoroughly creative occupation.

## Sampling

Sampling takes the technolgy of electronically stored sound one step further by offering a process whereby sound is recorded, stored digitally, and then manipulated via an electronic keyboard. In this way, sounds from nature can be transformed into instrumental voices, as can historical (or other) sound "bites."

## MIDI

All the products of one's own creativity—whether new sounds or fully orchestrated compositions—can be stored in a computer-compatible format. With the Musical Instrument Digital Interface, or MIDI, such data in the computer may be reworked, varied, and manipulated. The reproduction, for instance, of a piano piece in a fiendishly rapid tempo that

**111** A mixing console.

no human pianist can achieve, is just as easy as halving the tempo in only one voice or transposing a voice higher or lower. Even with computer-controlled technology, however, the human element remains a central part of musical expression. In ongoing efforts to bear this fact in mind, or perhaps to disprove it, programs have been developed that will insert slight rhythmic variations (pauses and quickenings) into otherwise metrically rigid computer-generated pieces. Thus, the original intention of music making as a human action has not been abandoned in MIDI-controlled keyboarding.

112 The violin maker needs the proper materials and tools and a well-trained eye.

single kind of instrument or of a closely related family of instruments. A violin maker may also make violas and cellos, just as a harpsichord maker may make clavichords. The instruments are produced in small workshops or factories that then guarantee the quality of their products. There are also large factories, often owned by much larger corporations, where instruments are mass-produced. Most of the violins, guitars, and pianos produced by these firms lack the individual tone quality of instruments made by hand. They are, however, perfectly fine for beginners and less ambitious amateurs.

## Craft as art

The development and construction of a musical instrument demands a great deal of artistry and an extraordinary amount of craftsmanship and skill on the part of the instrument maker. Further, he or she must be aware of the historical, acoustic, and aesthetic attributes of the instrument. Last, but not least, the instrument maker must possess sufficient musical understanding and playing proficiency to be able to check and evaluate the quality of the instrument.

Most instrument makers specialize in the production of a

## The secret of the violin

A glimpse into a violin workshop shows us something more than the many tools and different woods and finishes that go into making a violin: It quickly becomes clear that the construction of a violin—which, after all, consists of very few individual parts—must be a very complex process. The art of the violin maker consists chiefly in his or her ability to finish and fit together the individual parts of the instrument into an instrument that is visually convincing and beautiful and, of course most importantly, has beautiful tone. In order to do this, the violin maker must thin out the face at certain points, place the sound post and bass bar in just the right place, and perform all the other tasks with similar precision and care.

Mastering the art of violin making takes many years (112) and demands something more that cannot be explained by reason alone. Violins and similar instruments are coated with a varnish whose recipe remains the violin maker's secret. Of course, chemical analysis can reveal the ingredients of the varnish but, on the issue of the tonal changes it effects, such analysis can say nothing.

Thus, a violin can be viewed as a work of art, and can attain a value far beyond the cost of producing and marketing it. This is especially true of the instruments made by Andrea Amati (ca. 1500–1579) and Antonio Stradivari (1644–1737), whose violins still set the standard for beauty of tone and perfection of form— and are bought and sold for astronomical sums.

## Simple instruments?

Even very simple-looking instruments, if they are important to a certain kind of music or perhaps an entire music culture, are planned and made with as much care as more complex instruments. Spanish castanets (113), for example, do not require as many stages of preparation as violins, but the process of construction must be just as carefully carried out if the castanets are to be usable.

## Building an organ

Making an organ (115) requires tremendous material, technical, and personal resources. Each instrument is designed for the

113 Various steps in the production of castanets. The construction of this seemingly simple instrument requires care and craftsmanship.

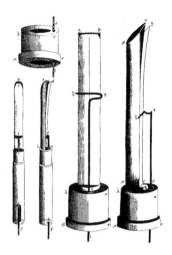

**114** As one of the final steps in the construction of an organ, the organ maker intones and tunes the pipes.

**115** The various parts of an organ—the main register, the *Brustwerk*, and the back positive—contain registers with different sound characteristics. Together they constitute the complete organ, or *organo pleno*, which is capable of producing a very complex sound.

specific room where it will be placed—normally a church or larger concert hall.

The architecture of the church interior influences the organ's acoustics and must therefore be included in the planning of the organ from the beginning. The disposition of the organ (the choice and arrangement of the registers) is normally determined jointly by an organist and the organ maker on the basis of the repertoire that will primarily be played on the instrument. In addition, the construction and design of the organ depend on the client's financial resources—if the organ is being built for a church community with dwindling resources, budgetary constraints must be factored into the design.

The organs produced by a given workshop usually have a characteristic tone that a professional will immediately recognize and that remains unchanged through a number of generations.

Three members of the Silbermann family became famous organ makers: Andreas (1678–1734), Gottfried (1632–1753), and Johann Andreas (1712–83). They produced important instruments in Saxony and later in Alsacia. Gottfried Silbermann, the brother of Andreas and uncle of Johann Andreas, was

# Instrument Making

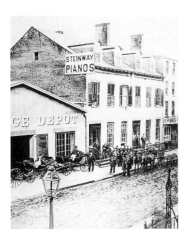

116 The workshop of Steinway & Sons, New York City, 1854.

also a piano maker and made important contributions to the development of the pianoforte (see p. 49).

In the 19th century, the French organ builder Aristide Cavaillé-Coll (1811–99) developed a new type of organ. His instruments, which number about 500, are particularly suited to the playing of French romantic music.

During the 1920s, the so-called organ movement demanded a reconsideration of the baroque tradition and attempted to replicate old instruments as described in Praetorius's *Syntagma musicum*. Through scientific errors, renovations of historical organs often caused more harm than good. Today, all kinds of organs are built, and historical instruments can be professionally restored: The process is quite expensive but it is also quite spectacular, as

117 The construction of a grand piano involves many steps.

# Instrument Making

can be seen in the reconstruction of the Arp-Schnitger organ in the Jacob's Church in Hamburg, Germany.

## Piano making

The production of an upright or grand piano is not nearly so extensive a project as making an organ. The earliest pianofortes were remodeled harpsichords, produced in small workshops. But the demand for pianos increased, leading to a pre-industrial production of the instrument. Heinrich Engelhard Steinweg immigrated to New York and, in 1853, founded the piano-making firm of Steinway & Sons (117). In 1880, a second factory was erected in Hamburg, Germany, to supply the European market. Because of their tonal qualities and high-quality craftsmanship, Steinway pianos have been the

instruments of choice of most pianists, and are to be found in all concert halls.

The process of making a grand piano is complicated and slow, but it is also comprehensible and within the grasp of the craftsman (117). With the exception of a few east Asian firms devoted to mass production, most piano firms produce on a manual rather than industrial basis.

## Instrument reproduction

Within the last two or three decades, reproduction and imitation of historical instruments have become increasingly important functions in the instrument-making world. To perform historical or early music as "authentically" as possible, many musicians choose to work with either restored original instruments or copies. Harpsichord makers in particular have worked intensively in this area. While early 20th-century imitations of period instruments were heavily characterized by construction techniques used in making modern instruments—for example, harpsichords were built with with iron frames and pedal registers—today's reproduction market strives to copy the period instrument exactly. The precision of replication is carried down to the most minute details—down to hand-forged joints if necessary. A general ex-

118 Many pianos retain the wing-shaped soundboard.

ception to all this historical accuracy is the substitution of quills made of flexible plastic for real quills, which simply wear out too quickly and are disproportionately expensive. The plastic proxies are designed to reproduce the properties of the natural articles.

Harpsichord makers are especially careful in the selection of strings. The tone of the instrument is chiefly determined by the material and characteristics of the strings, which should resemble those of the old models as exactly as possible. In order to produce such strings, the craftsperson turns to traditional methods of production. Even rather carelessly produced instruments attain an individual and brilliant tone when they are fitted with such strings.

In the 16th and 17th centuries, Antwerp, Belgium, became a center of keyboard instrument

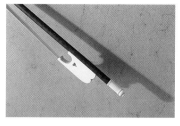

119  Some instrument makers specialize in reproducing historically accurate bows.

production. The Ruckers family led the harpsichord market with their semimodern production techniques. In the 18th century, the leading makers of French hapsichords were the family Blanchet and Pascale Taskin. Today, most harpsichord makers produce imitations based on Flemish and French models.

## Instrument building blocks

The trade with instrument components has become a secondary branch of instrument making. The consumer assembles "prefabricated" parts according to the instructions and—with some amount of craftsmanship—manages to produce a playable instrument. Such instrument kits are available for all kinds of instruments, including harpsichords,

120  The instrument maker does not usually do the painting and decoration of a harpsichord or a virginal.

**121** It is unusual for string instruments, such as these viola da gambas, to be so richly decorated.

clavichords, pianos, and, yes, even organs.

Another variation of instrument making serves a pedagogical purpose. In continuing education classes, seminars, youth programs and similar institutional programs, professional music makers oversee the creation of various kinds of basically usable instruments.

Building an instrument on your own, without using a kit, provides a learning experience that enhances both your interest in the instrument and your creativity.

Quite often the initial interest in building an instrument from scratch, or even with the help of finished parts, develops into a passion that can lead to a career. Unfortunately, for the person who finds him or herself caught up in the engrossing process of instrument making, the advantages of the master-apprentice system are lacking. And so the would-be instrument maker must be self-taught, or self-teaching, and perfect his or her craft alone. It is an arduous and challenging task.

## Master craftsmanship

Once upon a time, instrument makers were organized into guilds. Even today, the industry enjoys a certain degree of community spirit—though not unmixed with the spirit of competition and envy. Apprentices or journeymen and women who change firms or work independently after their training often remain in contact with their masters.

One can receive training in large firms such as organ factories or piano workshops, which are found everywhere. For string instruments, which are also made around the world in sites ranging from the one-person shop to the mass-production factory, the town of Mittenwald in Bavaria, Germany, and Cremona in Italy have shared a fine reputation for centuries.

## The art of instrument making

All instrument makers want their products to combine the technical demands of construction with an artistic and aesthetically pleasing form. This relationship between function and form tends to be particularly important for makers of musical instruments because instruments have a history of possessing a certain unquantifiable value that is independent of its market price.

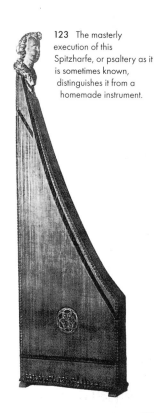

123 The masterly execution of this Spitzharfe, or psaltery as it is sometimes known, distinguishes it from a homemade instrument.

122 Many continuing education programs offer courses in making instruments. The final products usually have an acceptable appearance and tone.

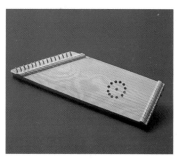

String Instruments

**124** Music is indispensible to festive occasions of every kind, but especially for dancing.

### Stretched strings

Unlike keyboard instruments whose complicated mechanisms are mostly hidden from the performer and the audience, string instruments are simply built and their mechanism for producing sound is much more direct and visible. When an audience in the concert hall is listening to acoustic (non-electrified) string instruments, they can watch the performers take their bows in hand, adjust the tension of the hairs, and play. If you sit close enough to a a cellist, for example, you may even be able to see the strings vibrating. Likewise, the sound-producing mechanisms of the favorite instruments of folk musicians are in plain sight and plainly understandable—from a campfire gathering singing along with a dulcimer to a folksinger in a coffeehouse who unpacks his guitar, tunes up, and starts to play. All of these instruments are not only mechanically simple, but portable as well, making them the favorites of street musicians, from the individual on a quiet (though hopefully resonant) corner under an eave to larger ensembles playing klezmer music in a city park. While even this seemingly informal mode of performance has today been graced with the advantages of electric amplification, as occasional street musicians drag along and unpack small amplifiers and generators to power the pickups in their acoustic guitars, the general impression of simplicity should not be mistaken for a lack of musical sophistication. Many a folk musician or street ensemble plays with great virtuosity and passion. And, despite the irresistible urge to add technology, technology, technology, many players of acoustic string instruments manage very well with very few technical accoutrements.

## The strings

Picture a violinist, or a cellist, the former poised with her instrument projecting proudly under her chin, the latter with her back straight and shoulders lifted for an up beat. With strong and confident gestures, they draw the bow across the strings, or with brisk staccato bounces, they skim the bow (**126**). Or, their bow resting in a closed grip, they pluck the strings with their index finger or with the pinky of the left hand to produce a "pizzicato." Among certain classes of musicians—classical symphony orchestra members, for example—the strings enjoy a particular position of esteem (is not the first violinist also called the concertmaster or mistress?), while world-famous soloists, Pablo Casals or Yo-Yo Ma on cello, Jascha Heifetz or Anne-Sophie Mutter on violin (to name two among many), command enthusiastic audiences for their concerts and

**125** Leopold Mozart (1719–87), father of Wolfgang Amadeus, wrote a violin study method that was highly regarded in his time.

**126** Nicolò Paganini (1782–1840) was one of the greatest violin virtuosi of his time.

String Instruments

**127** The violin assumed its signature shape in the mid-16th century. In the Middle Ages precursors of the violin were commonly used to accompany courtly song. This illustration depicts the Minnesinger Heinrich, also known as Frauenlob.

**128** Violins used in folk music are sometimes fancifully decorated.

**129** Violin scrolls are not usually as lavishly carved as the scrolls on their cousins, the gambas.

their recordings and become stars in their own right. This seemingly irrefutable prestige notwithstanding, cultural respect for string instruments and their players has fluctuated widely in the course of music history—from denigration of "fiddlers" (remember that early musicologists such as Virdung considered violins and other strings "useless"), to something akin to secular canonization with the Violons du Roy, the royal viols at the court of Louis XIV.

### From dance fiddle to violin

While the violin's musical use and repertoire has expanded from purely social dance accompaniment to a classical repertoire second only to that of the piano, the instrument itself has undergone

very few structural or technical changes. The external form has not changed fundamentally since the mid-16th century. This form integrates features of string instruments from different ages, including the medieval fidel, the lyra, and the rebec, the latter two of Arabic origin.

### Construction

The form of the violin is unmistakable (**128**). Its body (sound box) narrows in the middle and has two f-holes, one on either side of the strings. Attached to the body is a neck with a fretless fingerboard, which ends in a pegbox with a decorative scroll (**129**). At the lower end of the instrument's body, the tailpiece is fastened to the instrument with the end button. (The chin rest is a modern addition, for the violinist's comfort.) The violin's four strings, attached (by winding) to the pegs at

one end and to the tailpiece (with fine tuners) at
the other, stretch over a bridge (**130**). They are
tuned in intervals of a fifth, starting from the G below middle C, hence: G, D, A, and E (in standard
musical notation, this would be g-d$^1$-a$^1$-e$^2$).

Though not visible, the internal features of the
violin are critical for the production and quality
of tone. Between the top plate (belly) and the
back plate of the body is a soundpost, a thin
wooden rod (this designation may be a little confusing because, in other string instruments, it may
also refer to the wooden block into which the
scroll sticks). The soundpost (**131**) is attached in
one of the most sensitive places of the instrument
where it both transmits the vibrations from the
belly to the back plate and increases the general
stability of the body. The bridge, with the soundpost, also conducts the vibrations and thus is a
critical component in producing the instrument's
sound. The bridge stands on the belly plate on
two "feet," the "descant" (under the highest
string) and the "bass" (under the lowest). The
soundpost, inside the instrument, extends roughly
under the bridge's descant foot; the position is

130   Different shapes of
violin bridges.

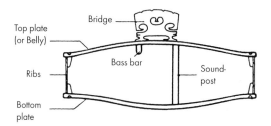

Top plate (or Belly)
Bridge
Ribs
Bass bar
Sound-post
Bottom plate

not exact because the bridge is moveable, but it
tends slightly more on the descant side. Under
the bass foot of the bridge is a small wooden
block called the "bass bar," which helps reinforce the deeper frequencies. The soundpost and
bass bar work together in the violin and other

131   The soundpost and bass
bar determine the sound of a
violin.

**132** Early bows, before the addition of the frog, used quite simple mechanisms to stretch the hair.

**133** The tightness of the bow is regulated by a screw at the frog end of the stick.

string instruments to balance the tone throughout the instrument's entire range.

The bow, which is drawn across the strings to set them vibrating, is composed of a flexible wooden stick strung with horsehair. To increase the friction of the horsehair against the string, and thus increase the sound, the player coats it with rosin. Since the 17th century, the horsehair has been attached to the stick by a "frog" (**132**) at the lower end of the bow, from which the player controls the bow. The hair tension can be adjusted with a screw mechanism at the frog.

## Change of musical function

In the course of the musicological development of the violin, from the time of the Middle Ages and Renaissance, the violin has more and more assumed the high part in ensemble playing, and has increasingly taken over the leading part. Musical details that could not be executed by other high instruments because of technical limitations, such as melodic ornaments that demanded precision, speed, and subtle tonal variation, allowed the violin to step into this role. Then, perhaps predictably, as the leading role of the violin grew more distinct, so, correspondingly, violin playing technique also developed, expanding the expressive possibilities of the instrument to include the finest musical nuances. For this reason, the violin demands earlier sophisticated ear training, since the absence of frets obliges the violinist to both find and determine the pitch and to modulate the quality of tone and sound by ear alone. The lack of frets is largely responsible for the popular impression that the violin is an extremely difficult instrument to play, and therefore that any capable violinist must possess uncanny ability. Even trained musicians (though perhaps not professionals) are prone to remark, "I can't believe anybody can play that thing!" In the orchestra, which since the 18th century has become a standardized ensemble with specific instruments playing different roles, the violins,

especially the first violins, are the leading group.

## The violin family

The name "violin" is a diminutive form of "viola," implying that it is the smallest member of an entire family of instruments (**134**). Through the entire pitch spectrum, from bass to soprano, instruments are built with different ranges which somewhat overlap. Again, the designation for these instruments is inexact, even though very familiar. The violin, also called the fiddle, takes the soprano voice; the viola (its full name is the viola da braccio, from the Italian for "arm") plays the alto; the violoncello (cello, for short) the tenor; and the double bass (contrabass) the bass register. The violoncello is the Italian name for a small form of the violone, which was a precursor to the contrabass and belonged to the gamba family (see below).

## Gambas

Now, to make the terminology thoroughly confusing, the name "viola da gamba" (*gamba* =

**134** The violin family: The contrabass (right) has a slightly different shape from the other instruments of the family, but it is usually included among them.

**135** Viola da gamba.

"leg" in Italian) is used for all viols that are held on or with the legs, and therefore is particularly used to denote the cello. Gambas, however, are an entirely separate instrument family, with their own range from bass to soprano in pitch. They differ from the violin family in body shape, and they also have fretted bridges and more strings. The baroque revival of the 1960s and 1970s made gambas popular once again. They appear in "authentic instrument" performances of nearly every baroque ensemble music.

### The gamba versus the violin

In their heyday in late 17th-century France, the gamba was both aesthetically and practically equivalent to the violin. Its role in the so-called consort, an ensemble with normally four instruments, was especially popular and allowed the players to produce particular tonal effects of great finesse, which captivated audiences. In the course of the 18th century, the interest in the gamba waned as enthusiasm for the violin waxed. While new interest in old instruments and their authentic playing techniques has revived interest in the gamba, it is still generally confined to early-music performances and specialized groups, though quite popular among musicians themselves.

Usually, gambists begin as cellists. In contrast to the cello, there is a considerable solo literature for the gamba. In consort (baroque ensemble) playing, the gamba sometimes plays the basso continuo line, but also often has more interesting contrapuntal lines.

Producing a consistent tone on the gamba is very difficult and requires prolonged study and

**136** The refined sound of the gamba is especially suited to solo playing.

**137** The *Partita in E-Major* by Johann Sebastian Bach is an important early solo violin work.

practice. To find the optimal sound, gambists experiment a lot with bow technique, string material, and playing position. Other differences from the cello include a different bow hold (the cello bow is held from above, the gamba from beneath); furthermore the gamba has no end pin and therefore must be held and stabilized by the player's knees, and the gamba is generally used to produce a straighter tone, without vibrato, than the cello. Because gambists are generally early-music specialists, they often possess an impressive scholar's knowledge of detail of old theoretical writings and sources.

**String repertoire**

String sounds are omnipresent today. Not only are they used to express saccharine, sentimental emotions (or what is taken for them), they are abused to this end. No romantic film, or even television commercial praising the sweetness of life, gets very far without the swelling of tremulous violins. On the other hand, classical violin music has a much more serious, sober reputation, and many composers wrote their most important works for this instrument. Around 1700, Arcangelo Corelli wrote masterful compositions for the violin and/or string orchestra that are still vibrant and exciting to hear today. The string quartet, comprised of the three higher-voiced members of the violin family (first violin, second violin, viola, and cello), became the dominant

**138** Henri Vieuxtemps (1820–81).

chamber music ensemble of the classical era. It was for such ensembles that the composers to end all composers wrote: Joseph Haydn originated the form, Mozart used it with brilliance, and Beethoven liberated it.

In the 19th century, music written for strings, especially for violins, began to demand a level of virtuosity that not even every professional violinist can satisfy. Perhaps the most important element of the 19th-century violin style is vibrato, a tremolo of the pitch produced by wiggling the finger from side to side while it presses the string. Composers of works demanding such technique were sometimes ridiculed as "hams," including Nicolò Paganini (whose own playing was so dazzling that he was rumored to be possessed), Pyotr Ilyich Tchaikovsky, Max Bruch, Henri Vieuxtemps (138), and Henry Wieniawski. In 20th-century music, violins are used mostly as ensemble instruments, though composers like György Ligeti, Krzysztof Penderecki, Karlheinz Stockhausen, Phillip Glass, and Arvo Paart have composed solo violin works.

The interrupted tradition of gamba music, which has been enthusiastically revived by the agents of historical authenticity, is represented through composers who wrote predominantly or exclusively for this instrument: Sainte Colombe, Marin Marais, Antoine and Jean-Baptiste Foqueray in France, Alfonso Ferrabosco, John Coperario, Tobias

**139** Elvis Presley, among many other early rock and roll musicians, helped make the guitar popular again.

Hume, and John Jenkins in England. Elsewhere, composition for the gamba has been more reserved and conventional.

**Plucked, not bowed**

Plucking the strings, which brings the player into direct contact with the instrument's vibrating parts, is the most common and popular method of playing string instruments around the world. Once we enter the world of plucked string instruments, we encounter a range of instruments, traditions, and techniques as varied as the history of music itself. This "group" must include the harpsichord, whose strings are plucked by quills, the bowed instruments when they are plucked for pizzicato, the guitar, the banjo, the dulcimer, and the washtub bass. Clearly, this group spans the globe in social context as well as technique.

One of the most commonly used plucked string instruments is, of course, the guitar, whether it is taught as a vocal accompaniment in schools, or picked up by a young person who wants to learn a few folk songs or imitate a rock star (139). Many music stores sell nothing but guitars, and many catalogs of children's toys and musical learning gear offer scaled-down guitars (ranging in quality from the useless toy to a decent instrument that can sustain its tuning and produce a reasonable tone) for young, small hands. The guitar is so popular because it is relatively

140 Electric guitars may have fanciful shapes, rather than the "classic" form of acoustic guitars.

141 The harp was a popular instrument of bourgeois music during the 18th and 19th centuries. It was often stereotyped as a "woman's instrument."

85

**142** Even in the Middle Ages different kinds of guitars were common. Illustration from the *Cantigas de Santa Maria*.

**143** A Flamenco dancer accompanied by guitar and clapping.

easy to play and because so many people are exposed to it. That it also has a long tradition as an instrument of art music is not so well known (though certainly the career of guitarists such as Andrés Segovia has gone a long way toward broadening perceptions of the instrument). Other plucked string instruments, such as a harp or a lute or, for that matter, a Bavarian zither, tend to be familiar only among certain esoteric circles:

the harp (**141**) by the concert-goer, the lute by the lover of early music, the zither by the folklorist.

That the plucked string instruments (with the exception of the guitar) are known as "art" instruments mostly by a small following is just an outgrowth of particular currents in western culture. This was not always the case in Europe, and in many non-western societies, plucked string instruments have long been at the center of musical culture.

## The guitar

By far the most popular plucked string instrument, the guitar is found in many musical arenas. Historians have suggested that it may be traced back to Babylonian, ancient Egyptian, and classical Greek forms, but there is no definitive proof of this lineage. The name "guitar," however, is clearly derived from the Greek kithara, which was a kind of lyre.

The guitar has a body (resonator or sound box) formed like a figure eight, with a long neck in relation to the body and a broad fingerboard which is crossed by 19 metal bands called frets. A striking external characteristic is the sound hole in the upper third of the body. Most guitars have six strings (some have twelve, comprised of six duplicate pairs, but in any case retain the same tuning as the six-string guitars). The strings are of nylon or steel, replacing the original gut strings, and are attached to the lower end of the instrument at a bridge; they run over the fingerboard to the screw plate where they can be tuned by mechanically turned pegs. The sound box is reinforced through the width of the ribs and inside with radiating posts, which

**144** In the triumphal procession of Emperor Maximilian I, as depicted by Hans Burgkmair in 1516, lute players, harpists, gambists, and wind players rode along.

not only stabilize the structure but, as in violins, influence the sound.

**145** Schematic plan of a lute.

### Concert, dance floor, campfire

The diversity of the guitar is exemplified by the very different uses of its musical and technical possibilities. It has figured in art music as well as in folk music for centuries. As early as the 16th century, the guitar technique of plucking a single melody—as was usual on the lute—was

**146** A Chinese pi-pa.

# The Lute: An Instrument of the World

**147** A Japanese shamisen.

**148** Indian sitar virtuoso Ravi Shankar. Shankar gained some popular notice in the west when he played with George Harrison of the Beatles, as well as with violinist Yehudi Menuhin.

used. To accompany dances and folk songs or, as in the old cliché, to serenade a fair maid, the guitarist strummed chords. While many a guitar player may confine him or herself to a narrow use of the instrument, absolute mastery requires learning the melodic (single-note plucking) technique. Chord strumming, on the other hand, may be used effectively after only brief practice. It fulfills fairly well the purpose which its simplicity suggests. Since the more basic musical demands of most Pop music are not very different from traditional techniques used for folk songs, it is not surprising that much Pop music adds little embellishment to this basic style of playing. Guitar virtuosity, however, may be found in various musical cultures. Flamenco music (**143**), which combines plucking and strumming, involves a virtuosity based on a Spanish folk and dance tradition, while popular guitarists from Chet Atkins to Eric Clapton, from David Wilcox or Patty Larkin to Mark Knopfler bring instrumental mastery to country-western, folk

music, and rock n' roll. Once the instrument of choice among the young, the electric guitar has matured as its best players have aged, and where many may hear only indistinct noise at a loud rock concert, many may also hear beauty.

## The lute: An instrument of the world

As the collective name of a group of instruments encompassing a multitude of differently formed instruments with a few common structural characteristics, the designation "lute" has been com-

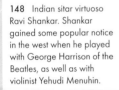

**149** The ud is one of the most important instruments of Arabic music.

mon since Hornbostel and Sachs. In one form or another, lutes may be found in nearly every culture around the world. In the Hornbostel and Sachs taxonomy, lutes are chordophones in which the vibrating string apparatus cannot be detached from the resonator without destroying the instrument (**145**). A secondary, but equally definitive characteristic is the parallel arrangement of the strings. Among the better-known instruments in this general category are violins, guitars, banjos, mandolins, balalaikas, and sitars, but there are many lesser-known instruments as well. They may be round-backed or flat-backed, fretted or fretless, bridged or bridgeless, use drones, have duplicate pairs of strings, be plucked, strummed, bowed, or played with a glass or metal tube, acoustic or electric: in short, an almost endless variety.

150 Many Renaissance paintings show angels playing a lute. This painting is by Vittore Carpaccio (1455–1525).

## Lutes in east Asia, India, the Middle East, and Europe

The different external forms of the lutes are as varied as the materials from which the instruments are built. The composition of any given lute, of course, is likely to be related to the natural environment in which it is built. Wood is often used because of its excellent natural resonance, while some kinds of gourds are also used as sound boxes. Often, animal hide is stretched over the resonator (as in the banjo).

Historically, the use of animal products may have had a religious significance: Some cultures hold beliefs that the animal's qualities are transferred to the instrument

151 A decorated mandolin.

String Instruments

89

String Instruments

152   A Russian balalaika.

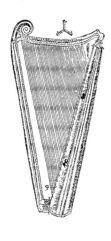

153   A harp, as illustrated by Michael Praetorius in the *Syntagma musicum*.

and so directly affect the player and the audience and enhance the power of the music to communicate with a deity. It is certainly common in western culture to use music for psychological effect.

The shamisen (**147**), a Japanese lute with cat-gut strings, usually accompanies songs and has a more "nasal" sound than most western lutes and guitars. A melody line is plucked with a large ivory plectrum, which adds a slight rasping sound.

The Indian sitar (**148**) has a bright, silvery, and extremely flexible sound. The strings are so flexible that pitches can be varied in fractions (microtones) rather than just in the half-step increments of western music. Indian and Arabic music use these microtones expressively.

From the Arabic lute, with its pear-shaped body, comes not only the western lute itself but also the name. *Al'ud* is Arabic for "the wood" (**149**). The similarity of "Al'ud" and "lute" is obvious: it has come to us in Italian as *liuto*, in French as *luth*, in English as *lute*, and in German as *Laute*.

Like the gamba, the lute enjoyed its European heyday in the 16th and 17th centuries, and then it began to fade from the musical scene. Also like the gamba, the 20th-century revival of interest in early music has renewed interest in the lute. In Arabic and Turkish musical traditions, the lute has never gone out of favor but has remained popular over the centuries.

### Mandolin, balalaika

The mandolin (**151**), another pear-shaped lute traditionally plucked with a quill plectrum, has a varying number of strings depending on its cultural origin. Early large mandolins had six to eight courses of single or paired strings, while the smaller instruments had only four or five. The popular instrument in the United States today is a four-coursed version, with paired strings (i.e., eight

  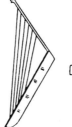 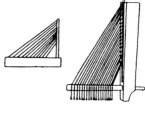

strings tuned in pairs).
Many classical composers wrote mandolin parts, e.g. Vivaldi, Telemann, Mozart, Verdi, Mahler and Schönberg. Thus, it may be found in orchestral formation along with accordians and contrabasses.

154 Different Egyptian harp forms.

One of the challenges of the mandolin, whether in classical arrangements or among folk-rock performers, is keeping the instrument in tune. Because of the paired-string arrangement, when the player plucks a note, it is played by two strings simultaneously. If these two strings are not exactly in tune with each other, then the instrument will sound noticeably out of tune. The mandolin player, therefore, must have a very well-trained ear and be able to tune the instrument deftly and frequently.

The balalaika (152), often considered synonymous with Russian folk music, has an exact triangular form. It has three strings, which can be tuned either in fourths or fifths, so that sometimes the highest and lowest string sound the same note an octave apart to enhance the sound. The balalaika tends to be built and played within families. Many people find the sound of the balalaika a bit melancholy.

## The harp

Harps (155) are chordophones; their strings run perpendicular to the soundboard (resonator)

155 European medieval harp.

String Instruments

and are attached to a frame. The player plucks the strings from both sides. This prosaic description actually names all the essential structural features of the harp and illustrates how it differs from other chordaphones. Such a simple structural design lends itself to many variant forms. And, indeed, many completely different harps exist that may be distinguished by the form of the frame on which the strings are stretched.

In western minds, the harp may be associated with religious or ritual music. But even in ancient times it was used on social occasions. The earliest known representations of harps are found among the Sumerians. These were "bow harps" whose bow-shaped frame suggests that the harp might have evolved from the hunting bow or the musical bow, with a resonator attached. How it migrated from the Tigris-Euphrates area to other regions is unclear, though we do know that it spread from Mesopotamia in one direction to India and East Asia and in the other direction to Africa. Like the bow-harp, the angular harp originated in Mesopotamia, though the history of its dissemination is unclear. All we can be sure of is that, after traveling eastward, it returned to Arabia and Turkey.

That instruments have migrated is not unexpected. As a piece of anthropological history, however, it is valuable. Since the origin of the harp is well known, some read this as proof that human civilization itself originated in the region near the Tigris and Euphrates Rivers. This remains merely a theory, however.

156  Celtic, or Irish, harp. To many, this is the archetypal instrument of traditional Irish music.

### The Celtic Harp

The 1960s and 1970s experienced a folk music and folklore revival that brought international interest in the Irish or Celtic harp. As Irish and Scottish folk songs were adopted into the repertoires of popular folksingers, they inspired widening

enthusiasm for the native instruments and musicians. The Celtic harp has existed since the 13th century virtually unchanged. The instrument is much smaller than the harp used in classical music and is often used in education, most likely because it is less expensive and easier to handle (156).

This harp was popular throughout Europe. Many paintings of the Middle Ages show the harp as an instrument of the nobility and the professional musician. It was also the instrument of the biblical King David and for this reason, if no other, highly esteemed. In time, the harp, along with many other instruments, was pushed aside and almost forgotten. The medieval form is played again today by musicians interested in reviving and reproducing antique music.

### In the orchestra

The development of the harp into an orchestral instrument, like that of many other instruments, was accompanied by mechanical progress. A screw mechanism for tightening and loosening the strings made it

**157** Like other instruments, harps were sometimes splendidly decorative.

**158** The qanun is an Arabic zither that is plucked with a plectrum.

**159** A hammered dulcimer player.

String Instruments

160 The langleik, a Norwegian zither.

possible to tune the harp chromatically (using the whole and half steps of the major and minor keys) and thus to play 18th- and 19th-century orchestral music (**157**). While early harp music was little more than a diversion for the salon, as the instrument gained in technical and tonal complexity, it gained appreciation among symphony composers. Berlioz used it in his *Symphonie fantastique* and was followed by 19th-century composers including Liszt, Richard Strauss, Sibelius, Ravel, and Debussy, and in the 20th century by Fauré and Saint-Saëns.

### The zither raises a smile

Hornbostel and Sachs classify the zither as a simple chordophone whose resonator may be removed without obliterating the nature of the instrument. Its most striking feature, however, is the method of playing it. The only difference between the Bavarian or the Appalachian hammered dulcimer, the Hungarian zimbalon, the Arabic and Indian santur music, on the one hand—leaving aside their exterior form—and the Alpine zither, the Arabic qanun (**158**), and the Finnish kantele, on the other, is that the former are played with hammers or mallets while the latter are plucked by the fingers or with a plectrum.

161 A Japanese koto.

### Arched boards

Some types of zithers have a flat floor and an arched top. Hornbostel and Sachs, not always philologically consistent in their terminology, called these polyheterochord instruments "arched board zithers." This type is common in different shapes in East Asia.

In Japan, the koto (**161**) is one of the most important instruments of traditional music. It is almost six and a half feet long and has 13 strings stretched over a movable bridge. The thumb, first, and second fingers of the right hand pluck the strings while the left hand depresses the strings behind the bridge and so alters the pitch. Playing the koto truly demands mastery of the instrument which can only be acquired through long and intense study.

## Music for plucked string instruments

The repertoire for plucked string instruments is naturally very diverse. For guitars, lutes, and harps, there are countless compositions from the Middle Ages to the present. In the early music of the Middle Ages and the Renaissance, these instruments were often used to accompany dances and songs. The "Intavolatura"—transcriptions of entire madrigals and other polyphonic song compositions for the lute—were very popular. Though this music was not written for the guitar, only minor changes are necessary to make it quite playable on that instrument; a good deal of lute music therefore has been transcribed for the modern guitar. There is no dearth of literature for the guitar, of course, but for more variety of expression in classical works, guitarists have often turned to lute music. Among composers of the classical period who wrote pieces specifically for guitar—much of it for civic, as opposed to symphonic occasions—are Maurizio Giuliani, Fernando Sor, Johann Kaspar Merz and the famous virtuoso violinist, Nicolò Paganini.

The 20th century brought a sort of reversal of fortune for guitar music, especially in Spain where the guitar had always been popular. The "Concierto d'Aranjuez" of Joaquin Rodrigo is often played today. Elsewhere, modern "art music" composers, such as Benjamin Britten and

**162** The lyre is associated with ancient Greece. The word "lyre" is used for other string instruments, which may have little in common with the original lyre, such as the "Drehleier"—a hurdy-gurdy.

Hans Werner Henze, have also turned to this instrument.

Nowhere is the dual role of the guitar as an instrument of art and folk music more clear than in Spanish music. The countless tangoes and other dances, whose kinship with Arabic music is apparent, are as a rule orally (or manually), rather than formally, transmitted. This is typical of the repertoire of instruments used predominantly in folk music.

In Arabic music, qanun and santur players are known for their skillful improvisations on set melodic models, which are characteristic for this music. For Indian music, instruments need to be extremely flexible in terms of both tone quality

**163** Jan Brueghel, *Allegory of Hearing*. This painting (ca. 1620) shows almost all the instruments in use in western Europe at the time. Of course, the arrangement of the instruments has nothing to do with current musical practice.

and pitch. Plucked string instruments are well suited to the task. The performance of ragas, in which artful and rhythmically complex melodic improvisations follow a given basic model, are especially effective on the northern Indian sitar, as well as on other instruments with flexible tonal possibilities.

In East Asian music, lutes are often used to accompany songs. The repertoire for the Japanese koto has changed greatly in the course of a long tradition. This instrument's sonorous sound fascinates many western listeners, who often use koto music for meditation, which in Japan is one function, though by no means the only purpose, of the music.

**164** In the 19th century, many musicians were subject to caricature.

## Music is for listeners

Music is an extremely complex art form. Unlike the visual arts and written (as opposed to dramatic) literature, where the viewer or reader—the consumer—is in a direct relationship with the work of art, music requires some vehicle of communication, which means a process of musical interpretation. The acoustical realization of music, whether a work of grand art or an unprepossessing folk tune, is a form of communication between part-ners in two very different roles. The musicians present a composition, the audience listens and then indicates pleasure, displeasure, or indifference.

## Grouping variations

Throughout the history of music, various styles and forms have been developed for specific instruments and group arrangements. Here, one can distinguish three different variations: solo playing on an instrument capable of harmony, solo playing with accompaniment, and ensemble playing (from a duet to a symphony orchestra).

## The piano

From his or her very first piano lesson, the student begins to learn how to play a music piece as completely and perfectly as the instrument allows, or demands. In other words, the piano student must grapple with the entire piece, while a violin player or a flautist may be concerned with only a single part of a piece that will be played together with others. Most

**165** The Mozart family at play: father Leo-pold, son Wolfgang, and daughter Nannerl.

piano compositions are, in fact, meant to be played as solos. This offers certain benefits to the pianist. Each player can choose pieces suited to his or her technical abilities and work toward playing them in a musically intelligent way, and is ultimately the lone arbiter of the taste to be shown in interpretation. A Bach two-part invention or a Haydn minuet, a short piece from Robert Schumann's *Album für die Jugend* (Album for Youth) or from Béla Bartòk's *Microcosmo* is not essentially any different from Beethoven's "Hammerklavier" sonata or the "Etudes d'Exécutions transcendentes," the progressively more difficult piano studies by Franz Liszt.

166  The Russian composer Sergei Rachmaninov was also a piano virtuoso.

## Virtuosos

For many pianists, the virtuosity of a piece—a quality that is completely unrelated to its musicality—is most important. The pianist—whether she or he likes it or not—has assumed the popular persona of a virtuoso (166). This image of the musician with unbounded technical ability was born in the 19th century and is one of the most persistent popular notions still today. Technical virtuosity will carry the pianist a long way, but, in a very practical sense, virtuoso pianists are also a dime a dozen. Technique is, then, a foregone conclusion—any serious pianist must command seemingly limitless piano technique, but to distinguish oneself from the crowd and build a successful career, one also needs a certain ineffable quality known as musicality.

## Piano concerti

A pianist's virtuosity may assume musicality and expressive clarity when he or she performs a piano concerto with orchestral accompaniment. The interplay between the piano and the symphony orchestra can produce glorious music. Even the giants of the genre, often just showcases for the piano virtuoso, possess a charm all their own. The concerti of Pyotr Tchaikovsky, especially the *First Concerto in B Minor*, and of Sergei Rachmaninov are excellent examples.

# Soloists and Ensembles

167 A typical ensemble of the baroque period.

## Organists and harpsichordists

The repertoire for organists and harpsichord players is also largely a solo canon. The character and stature of such musicians in the public eye, however, is quite different from the stereotype of the pianist. Organ music is usually performed as a part of a church service, specifically at the beginning and the end of the service. Organ concerts in which virtuoso solo works are performed also take place in church (since that is where most of the organs are!). Such musical activities are usually organized by the members of the church congregation and appeal to only a limited public.

With harpsichords, in the last 20 years interest in historically authentic playing has grown in direct proportion to traditional musical practice. Most such historical performances take place during summer festivals—in Europe, often in the halls of castles and palaces—and draw a large audience. Harpsichordists are likely to appear both as soloists and as accompanists, often presenting with various orchestrations a narrow slice of the baroque repertoire.

## One part with accompaniment

String and wind instruments—in short, all instruments capable of carrying a melody—are usually accompanied by a keyboard instrument or are played in ensembles. The violin is quite special in this regard, in that it has always been versatile as both a solo and an ensemble instrument. Since around the beginning of the 17th century, the violin has been the leading melodic instrument in the orchestra; it also earned a reputation as a highly virtuoso solo instrument played against a basso continuo accompaniment. Early composers such as the Austrian Johann Hein-

168 Violin virtuoso Anne-Sophie Mutter (b. 1963).

# Soloists and Ensembles

**169** Violin virtuoso Joseph Joachim (1831–1907).

rich Schmelzer (ca. 1620–80) and the Bohemian Heinrich Ignaz Franz von Biber (1644–1704) gave violin music its first boost. Within a single generation, the violin concerto developed into an important genre that demanded more and more technique and musicality from the soloist. At the same time, the violin continued to be an important ensemble instrument.

## Violin virtuosi

Like piano music, violin music has become a virtuoso art form. As social phenomena, the two are entirely comparable. With certain exceptions, virtuosi on other instruments do not enjoy the same popularity as violin soloists. Young talented violin players are hungrily hailed as prodigies, and mature violinists—like tennis and other sport figures—may well become the nucleus of a cult following.

## Forms of ensembles

Although set configurations of ensembles are Johnny-come-latelies in the history of music, instruments have always been matched up with other instruments on the basis of similar or opposite tonal qualities. In the 15th century the popular combination made up of shawm, pommer, and trombone was anointed with the title *alta musica* ("high music"). Combinations of every kind of plucked string instruments, such as harps, lutes, and psalteries, were favorite ensembles.

### *Cori spezzati*

Combinations of string and wind instruments are especially capable of variation when they are, for example, separated from each other to produce a double choral or echo effect, one of the innovations of Venetian music of the early 17th century. Giovanni Gabrieli (1553–1612), organist at Saint Mark's cathedral in Venice, used this *cori spezzati* (split chorus) technique especially effectively.

**170** An ensemble with harp, lute, and psaltery.

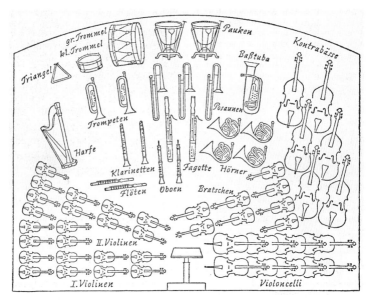

171 The seating arrangement of the modern symphony orchestra.

His student Heinrich Schütz (1585–1672) adopted and continued the technique in his own choral work.

### Solo—*Tutti*

The principle of alternation between two instrumental groups or a soloist and the body of the ensemble or orchestra (*tutti*) is a chief characteristic of baroque orchestra music. The interplay enlivens the even-tempered music made up of the similar tones produced by a string orchestra. The grouping of two violins, a viola, a violoncello (cello), and a contrabass originated in Italy and became the standard form. Simultaneously, in France, the orchestra became established as a five-body string

section with a wind trio—two oboes and a bassoon—along with the continuo.

### Three parts

Early chamber music also preferred stable instrumental groupings. From this preference came trio sonatas with either two violins, a cello, and either harpsichord or organ (to which a lute might sometimes be added). The wind version of this arrangement consisted of two oboes, a bassoon, and a continuo instrument. Of course, baroque musicians also combined violins, oboes, and flutes and played single parts with multiple instruments—baroque artists were generally quite free from constraints in making such arrangements.

## Classical orchestral organization

As continuo instruments, the harpsichord and the organ have always had the job to harmonically round out the three voices of a trio sonata. When the continuo form fell out of fashion, the viola assumed the role of providing harmonic wholeness. The use of similarly constructed instruments within the same family also created a homogeneity that began to approach the tonal understanding of the classic. Thus, at the end of the 18th century, the string quartet to some extent became the ideal instrumental configuration. For many composers

172  The banjo and guitar complement each other well.

173  An oboist plays a dance in the open air.

and musicians, this remains true today.

## Constancy and variation

The tendency toward a set combination of prescribed instruments is not an exclusive phenomenon of the culture of western music. Many non-European styles also rely on standard combinations of instruments. The music of India has many string and wind instruments in established arrangements; they are always played together with drums, which are necessary to create a comprehensible whole. In northern India, the drum pair of tabla and bayan and, in southern India, the double drum known as the mrdangam are typical.

Contemporary western music, in fact, no longer clings to a set ensemble form. On the contrary, the originality of many compositions often demands wholly individual instrumental groupings to express a musical statement.

**174** Prehistoric people made the first flutes from bones.

## Elementary musical experience: The wind instruments

The history of wind instruments offers its own slant to general inquiry into the origins of music and instruments, into their age and their functions. Unlike the hunting bow—itself an archaeological artifact that was transformed into a musical bow through the combination of two different elements (bow and gut), many tubular objects such as reeds, bamboo, and animal bones occur in nature. Without further processing, these tubes will produce musical pitches if someone blows into them in the correct manner. Almost everyone has experimented with the ordinary process of controlled exhalation, by whistling, by blowing across the mouth of a bottle, by blowing through the open end of a key or against a blade of grass. If we imagine the evolution of a certain vein of sound production starting with this simple process, which may even be performed unconsciously, a logical next step might be to drill holes in that reed or bone, just as one might fill the bottle (or some ancestral container) to vary the pitch produced by blowing. To do so, however, represents quite a developmental leap, conceptually beyond the vascillating function—music versus hunting utensil—of the ancient or prehistoric bow. Yet, according to evidence from the Stone Age unearthed by archaeologists, humans took this decisive step very early (**174**).

## The breath of the soul

The wind instrument involves the human body of the player in a uniquely intimate way, for it is the human breath—controlled by the diaphragm, the trachea, the throat, the mouth, the tongue, and the lips—that sets the air column of a wind instrument in motion. Even the immediacy of touch and sound that characterizes a pianist, a violinist, or a drummer at work is not quite as deeply personal, whether from a metaphorical/spiritual perspective, or from an utterly physical/physiological point of view, as this use of the individual's breathing mechanism (175).

The wind instrument and the wind instrument player are thus most like singers, in that the capacity to create music is inseparable from the ability to control a basic bodily function, and to combine it with the cerebral and emotional components that produce musicality. Some cultures believe that the singing voice is an extension, or expression, of the supernatural and/or divine, and wind instruments as a group come closest to the aesthetic ideal of the song (178).

This discussion takes us in fact into a realm of metaphysics that is not much a part of contemporary western beliefs or musical practice. We tend, rather, not to treat wind instruments—

**175** Aulos player and cymbal player. In ancient Greece the aulos, a double oboe, was played mostly at festivals and holidays, such as those of the Dionysus cult. Plato and Aristotle both scorned the instrument and blamed its sound for its listeners' depraved behavior.

Wind Instruments

whether a simple plastic recorder used to teach music to young schoolchildren (176) or instruments played with virtuosity either solo or within an orchestra—as something quite so elemental. Indeed, we

**176** Children enjoy experimenting with musical instruments at an early age. Recorders are particularly popular in early music education.

177 A "Bull-roarer." By spinning the piece of wood, which is fastened with a rope to the staff, this instrument produces a variable howling tone.

may readily call to mind the big brass bands, often on the march, whose members' cheeks are swollen and whose instruments drip with saliva. Hardly a metaphysical experience! But these are merely impressions and stereotypes.

### Aerophones and other wind instruments

In Hornbostel and Sachs's classification according to the mechanism of tone generation, instruments in which the air is set in motion without passing over a reed are called free aerophones. These include some obscure instruments such as the thunder stick, or bull roarer (177), a thin, flat piece of wood attached by a cord to a stick that is swung to produce a whirring sound, as well as the instruments we think of as the true wind instruments.

Hornbostel and Sachs further distinguished among these wind instruments, or aerophones, according to the structural features of the mouthpiece. These categories have entered most languages as standard terms:

—**Flutes**: The airstream meets with a cutting edge.
—**Oboes**: The air causes a double reed (two reeds placed next to one another) to vibrate.
—**Clarinets**: A single reed vibrates.
—**Trumpets**: The player's lips send air directly through a cup-shaped mouthpiece.

### The flutes

The flute tends to be a universally appealing instrument. They are popular in early music education because young people can play

178 An angel with a wind instrument. The image of angels playing music has been common since the Middle Ages.

pieces, or a "tune," with only a little instruction, and this ability to make progress may motivate the learning to continue.

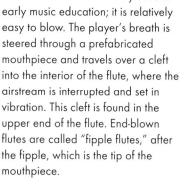

A special type of flute sometimes called a "flutophone" or "tonette" is commonly used in early music education; it is relatively easy to blow. The player's breath is steered through a prefabricated mouthpiece and travels over a cleft into the interior of the flute, where the airstream is interrupted and set in vibration. This cleft is found in the upper end of the flute. End-blown flutes are called "fipple flutes," after the fipple, which is the tip of the mouthpiece.

**179** A recorder made of ivory was something very special in the baroque period.

### The recorder

Recorders meet the foregoing description: They are fipple flutes. They are usually manufactured in two parts: the mouthpiece, which ends in a "block" or swollen joint, and the real flute, which has a number of holes that the player covers and uncovers to determine the pitch (the more holes covered, the longer the inner column of air and hence the lower the pitch) (**180**).

Various kinds of recorders are found in many different musical cultures around the world. Their variety is matched only by their universal attractiveness. In Europe, the recorder reached a peak during the baroque period, when it progressed from a Renaissance instrument usually played in ensemble into a solo instrument. The Italian designation *Flauto dolce* ("sweet flute") is a perfect expression of musicians' feelings about the sound of the recorder.

Interest in the recorder began to decline at the beginning of the 18th century. It was revived, however, in the 20th century when

**180** Examples of carved wooden recorders from the baroque period are also rare.

Wind Instruments

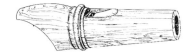 

**181** A drawing of a recorder's mouthpiece, showing the fipple on the right.

**182** This depiction of a recorder player implies that playing this instrument can be extraordinarily pleasant.

interest and theory in early music education grew. By the 1950s, it was often the instrument of choice for musical education in American public school systems. Like many other instruments (including the gamba, the Celtic harp, and others), the recorder benefited in the 1960s from the spurt of interest in authentic early music—that is, music from before 1800. What began as a fad developed into a stable offshoot of the serious music world. Not only have "authentic" period recorders and other early instruments found a booming market, but many areas have established regular outlets for early music players and lovers. Boston, for example, has become a center for early-music performance and instrument building. The annual Boston Early Music Festival brings together performers, instrument makers, and scholars from around the world.

The recorders on the market today range from extremely high-quality wooden recorders crafted by hand in small workshops to passable plastic children's recorders mass-produced and sold in music and toy shops.

### The flute as we know it

The flute known today from orchestra and chamber music concerts has inhabited its current form for about 150 years. It is made completely of metal and has a complicated system of clappers and pads that extends the player's ability to open and shut the holes that determine pitch. On a flute whose lowest pitch is middle C, it would be a difficult if not impossible stretch for most human hands to close the finger holes without this mechanism. Theobald Boehm, a German flautist, goldsmith, and ironmaster, developed the basic mechanized system still used today on the flute and other woodwinds, except the bassoon, between 1832 and 1850. The standard modern flute is called the Boehm flute (**183**) in his honor. Though made of metal, the flute is included in the "woodwind" group of instruments because it was once made of wood, before Boehm redesigned it.

**183**  The mouth hole on the Boehm flute is normally made of the same material as the rest of the instrument—silver or silver-plated metal.

**184**  Even a softly played flute can drown out a clavichord.

The mechanization of the flute masks the fact that the basic method of tone production has remained the same for millenia. The airstream is blown against a cleft, where it divides and sets the column of air inside the flute vibrating. In contrast to the recorder, however, the player must direct the airstream exactly across the mouthpiece in order to produce a tone. For this reason, considerably more training and practice are necessary to reach a comparable performance level on the Boehm flute than on the recorder.

# Wind Instruments

**185** *Principes de la flûte traversière*, by Jacques Martin Hotteterre (ca. 1680–1761). Hotteterre's method of study helped the transverse flute take precedence over the recorder in France.

**The *flûte traversière***

The precursor to the modern Boehm flute was made of wood and lacked a padded fingering mechanism (187). It was known as the "transverse flute" because it was the first flute to be held sideways to the body rather than in front like the recorder. From the mid-17th century it was built with a cover at the lower end. To produce a true intonation, the player must use a partially forked grip and, if necessary, turn the instrument slightly, which changes the pitch a little.

Like its metal successor, the transverse flute yields a soft, round sound that was very popular, particularly in baroque music. The transverse flute was especially popular at the beginning of the 18th century. All the leading composers of the time wrote for this instrument.

The flute was especially suited to be an ensemble instrument; its sound blended very well

**186** This famous painting by Adolph von Menzel (1815–1905) shows Frederick the Great of Prussia at the flute concert in Sanssouci.

with other instruments of the time, such as the gamba and the harpsichord, and with the violin. As an instrument of court music, it enjoyed great respect among the music-loving nobility, not least because of the influence of Frederick the Great of Prussia (186), himself a passionate flautist

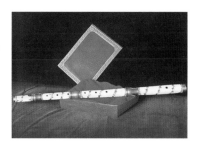

187 This transverse flute made of china is beautifully decorated but its musical range is limited.

who prompted the best composers of his time to compose works for flute (and who himself composed a series of appealing concertos). Among the music-loving middle class of the same period, the transverse flute also enjoyed great popularity.

## Notched flutes

Flutes that are cut to have a notched opening are not common in western music. Outside the western world, however, they are widespread. This type of flute is familiar to Americans through South American folk musician groups, and was popularized by the pop singer Paul Simon when he worked with native South American and African musicians. The quena of the Andes is made from a piece of a certain type of reed pipe with a knot at the lower end through which a hole is bored. Its sound is light and works best against a background of other instruments.

188 A South American quena.

## All nuance—The shakuhachi

The shakuhachi is a small end-blown notched flute from Japan. It is primarily used in meditation. Its

**189** The posture of the shakuhachi player shows that he is meditating on the instrument.

standard length is 21.8 inches. The precise length comes from a Chinese measurement, from which the instrument takes its name. It has four finger holes on the front and one on the reverse for the thumb. Its basic mode is the pentatonic scale, which corresponds to the notes $d^1$-$f^1$-$g^1$-$a^1$-$c^2$. (This is the scale that westerners recognize as typically Chinese and Japanese in sound. Playing a song on only the black notes of the piano will give the right sound.)

The particularities of the grip method—including half opened holes and an incredibly differentiated blowing technique—allow the musician an almost infinite range of tonal nuance. The production of nuance is a part of the philosophical understanding of shakuhachi playing, which is a process of breathing meditation with the help of tones (**189**). So, in shakuhachi music, the sound of the breath is almost as important as the notes themselves. The "moving-breath-become-sound" is set out in the "honkyoku," pieces which are designed to renew themselves repeatedly.

Playing the flute became fully ritualized over the course of centuries, in accordance with its social rank and symbolic character. Since the

**190** A shakuhachi is stored in a special silk pouch.

**191** Jacob van Oostzanen,
*Birth of Christ*, ca. 1512.
Depiction of musical angels.

19th century it has been used increasingly as an ensemble instrument and is sometimes included in contemporary art music.

## Flute music

The worldwide dissemination of the flute—played in Japan for meditation, in South America as a typical folk music instrument, and in Europe both as a child's first instrument and in many areas as a virtuoso instrument—has naturally been accompanied by the accumulation of an abundant and diverse repertoire.

The practice of *colla parte*—playing along with a voice part in an ensemble—was prevalent in the Renaissance until the recorder and transverse flute developed into solo instruments. Baroque music includes countless sonatas for flute and basso continuo (an accompanimental pattern played on a gamba or cello and filled in harmonically by harpsichord), and almost as many trio sonatas and concerti for these instruments. Joachim Quantz served at the Prussian court of Frederick the Great, where he was the authority on transverse flute. In France, Jacques Martin Hotteterre was his counterpart.

During the classical and romantic periods, the recorder was neglected and the flute appeared

**192** Claude Debussy
(1862–1918).

Wind Instruments

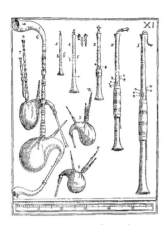

194 Wind instruments from the *Syntagma musicum* of Michael Praetorius.

only in orchestras. At the turn of the century and in the early 20th century, interest in the flute increased, and pieces appeared for solo flute and chamber works with flute. The *Syrinx* of Claude Debussy (192) and the *Sonata for Flute and Piano* of Francis Poulenc belong today to the standard repertoire.

**Vibrating reeds: Oboes and clarinets**

Hornbostel and Sachs included oboes and clarinets in a single instrument group under the heading of "shawms." Some quibble over the appropriateness of grouping them together, but the confusion of terminology is really only superficial. The two kinds of instruments are easily enough dis-

194 Bagpipes are among the so-called open-air instruments especially suited to dance music.

tinguished: Instruments with a double reed that vibrates in the mouth or inside a "wind capsule" are oboes; those with a simple reed fastened on a mouthpiece are clarinets.

**Bagpipes, crumhorns, and shawms**

Many instruments are associated with a certain country, ethnic group, or social class—perhaps no instrument more so than the bagpipe, ever and instantly evocative of Scotland. Folklorists know, however, that Irish music also uses a kind of bagpipe in which the bag is not filled by blown breath but inflated with a pumping movement of the arm. Moreover, anyone who

**195**  This bagpipe is an especially beautiful example of a "goat."

travels to the Balkans and comes in contact with local musical instruments will learn that here, too, are different varieties of bagpipes. The designation of *bagpipe*—the German word *Dudelsack* has an equally disparaging ring to it—in the musical culture of the Balkans has no such pejorative flavor. The Balkan bagpipes are often called simply *gajda* or *gajta*, probably from the Slavic word for goat, since the bags are made out of goat hide.

Bagpipes, played with a double reed, are voiced so that they simultaneously play two pitches in constant interval relationships, usually fifths. The melody pipes play the tune against this "drone." Some claim the bagpipes have a special appeal when the drones are played out of tune (which happens often enough).

Crumhorns (**196**), cornetti (from the Latin *cornus*, for horn) and shawms, depicted in the instrumental writings of the Renaissance, are also classified among the double-reed instruments, though they were all used in quite different musical contexts. Crumhorns and cornetti (the singular is cornetto) are soft-sounding instruments suitable for domestic

Wind Instruments

**196**  Crumhorns are not horns but oboe instruments. The double reed of a crumhorn is housed in a perforated cap.

**197** Left to right: Oboe, oboe d'amore, and an English horn. Oboes come in families like the string instruments. The individual instruments, however, have special forms and names.

**198** The modern oboe d'amore has kept its oval bulge at the bottom. The origin of its name is unknown.

**199** Edgar Degas (1834–1917), *The Opera Orchestra*. In the center is a bassoon.

use. Shawms, on the other hand, are loud and sharp and thus best suited to the open air.

### The oboe

The development of the oboe (**197**) in Europe has been similar to that of the flute. During the baroque, it experienced a heyday, though of a less prominent nature than that of the transverse flute.

Also like the flute, the oboe was only later fitted with a key and clapper system to guarantee precise intonation, which is unusually difficult on baroque instruments that are regulated essentially through the use of the breath. The oboe has a somewhat nasal tone color, which, however, is very flexible. While the oboe may stand out somewhat in small ensembles, in large orchestras it adds depth and color to the sound, particularly in combination with the flute.

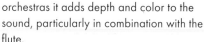

### The bassoon

The bassoon is the foundation of the double-reed instruments; in the orchestra it plays in the deep registers. It has a coiled tube that is approximately 92 inches long, giving it the length acoustically necessary to produce the lowest pitches, which begin at $_1B^b$ and end at e flat$^2$. As one of the common basso continuo instruments of baroque music, it was very popular. Later, however, it shared the fate of the other double-reed instruments

and is now used almost exclusively as an orchestral instrument, in which role it effectively rounds out the sound of the other reeds (**199**).

## Shanai and zurna

Oboes are much more common in Turkish, Arabic, and Indian music than they are in European music. The words *zurna* (**200**) for the Turkish and *shanai* (**201**) for the Indian instrument are actually linguistically related. Through the great migrations of people and cultures, some intangible goods— languages, philosophies, religions, traditions—have been transported as well, and so have movable goods, such as musical instruments. From India, the oboe has wandered west and spread throughout the Near and Middle East.

The shanai and the zurna have the nasal sound of all oboes, though theirs is a sharper tone than produced by the western instruments. The zurna is usually played in large parties along with a drum called a davul.

**200**  In Turkey, the oboe zurna is played together with the drum davul. In this picture the oboe recedes somewhat into the background. Its sound, however, stands up quite well against the drum.

Wind Instruments

**201**  The Indian oboe shanai has the typical nasal sound of all oboes.

117

**202** The Albert Schweitzer Brass Quintet: flute, bassoon, horn, oboe, and clarinet.

**203** A tenor saxophone.

## Oboe music

The oboe repertoire ranges from the simply structured melodies of Scottish bagpipe music to the small pieces of Renaissance dance music, to the solo and ensemble music of the baroque, and up to the highly ornamental melodies of Indian music.

The oboe generally produces a flexible tone that is suggestive, even to the untrained ear, of Indian music, while Scottish bagpipe music takes some getting used to before the pieces can be differentiated. Among the more classical western musical canon, Johann Sebastian Bach wrote especially beautifully for oboe, both as a solo instrument and as an obligato for the voice and other instruments; oboes play a prominent role in the score of his *St. Matthew Passion*, a masterwork of western music. Later, 19th- and 20th-century English composers such as Ralph Vaughan Williams, Frederick Delius, and Benjamin Britten have written effective plaintive melodies for the oboe. Mozart wrote magnificent "Divertimenti" for groups of wind instruments, including oboes and bassoons, which he also used very sensitively in his operas, especially *Cosi fan tutte*. The 20th century has witnessed the growth of an adventurous repertoire for the woodwind quintet (oboe, clarinet, flute, bassoon, French horn **202**).

The sound of the classic European oboe, played predominantly in the orchestra, is easy to identify. It is sometimes used to evoke a pastoral mood. There are relatively few solo oboe pieces and/or oboe works with piano accompaniment. Robert Schumann's *Märchenbilder* (Fairy Tale Pictures), op. 120, are

**204** A modern clarinet.

among the known compositions, along with a sonata by Francis Poulenc.

## The reed's the thing— Clarinets

The clarinet did not follow the typical developmental pattern of other instruments, most of which gradually changed their external form and became more mechanized. Around 1700, Johann Christoph Denner made a decisive structural change in the chalumeau, a French wind instrument, and thereby practically "invented" the clarinet. The chalumeau (from the Latin *calamus*, for reed) is indeed a reed instrument, which outwardly resembles a baroque recorder, but instead of a fipple-type mouthpiece, it has a vibrating reed. This instrument had a relatively narrow pitch range and could not be "overblown."

Overblowing is an acoustic peculiarity of many wind instruments whereby the player can use the fingering of a fundamental pitch in its range to play a higher pitch of that fundamental pitch's natural overtone series—that is, an octave, a fifth, or a third—by blowing harder. Denner's "invention" was a "speaker key" that enabled the chalumeau to produce these higher "overblown" pitches. The modified instrument was named the clarinet (from the Latin *clarus*, for clear or bright) because of its brilliant high notes. (The first written record of its performance in America comes from Benjamin Franklin, who wrote about a 1756 concert in Bethlehem, Pennsylvania, "Good musick, the organ accompanied with violins, hautboys, flutes, clarinets, etc.")

Theobald Boehm's fingering system for the flute was also suited, with some modifications, to the clarinet, which was a more popular solo

205 Traditionally, clarinets were fashioned out of different kinds of wood.

206 Contrabass clarinet

# Wind Instruments

## Adolphe Sax's Invention

Wind Instruments

**207** Legendary jazz saxophonist, Charlie Parker (1920–55).

**208** Sardinian launeddas.

instrument in the classical and romantic periods than either the flute or the oboe. The clarinet's tone can also be changed dramatically by the player's embouchure (mouth and lip position) so that, for example, one can play a smooth glissando (sliding pitch).

The wide pitch range of the clarinet is subdivided into three clearly distinguishable registers, of which the lower, the so-called chalumeau register, has a characteristically round, full quality. The higher register possesses tonal possibilities that allow expression of almost any emotion. This flexibility makes the clarinet well suited to jazz. Benny Goodman, whose heyday was in the "swing" era of the 1930s and 1940s (though he kept playing almost until his death in 1986) was probably the most famous American jazz clarinetist. The clarinet is also a staple of Klezmer music, the traditional music of the Jews in the shtetls of eastern Europe.

### Adolphe Sax's invention

Originally conceived of as an instrument for military bands, the saxophone, developed around 1840 by the Belgian Adolphe Sax and named after him (**203**), is now primarily used in a musical style Sax himself had never heard or (probably) imagined: jazz. While the saxophone appears in some 19th-century symphonic music, not all musicians agree that it is a good addition to this repertoire. Debussy was commissioned by a wealthy American woman saxophonist to write a sonata for the instrument, but never wrote it and kept the fee. The conductor Arturo Toscanini once said, "If all the saxophones in the world were laid end-to-end, it would be a good thing."

The saxophone is a horn-shaped metal instrument with a clarinet mouthpiece. Its playing technique is simpler than the clarinet's, and its register is narrower. The expressive tonal possibilities of the high register in the clarinet instrument group, which appear inexhaustible in the saxophone, make it especially suitable as a solo instrument. This is especially true in jazz, which as an improvisatory musical style, depends heavily on the inventiveness and personality of the soloist.

209  A launeddas player.

## A drone and two pipes—The Sardinian launeddas

This odd and obscure instrument is "like a bagpipe without the bag" (**208**). It is a triple single-reed instrument with three cane pipes, two of which have finger holes while the third acts as a drone.

The player takes all three pipes into his or her mouth and uses "circular breathing" to produce a continuous tone on the drone pipe and a melody on the smaller pipes (**209**). Circular breathing, which in other music cultures has a philosophical basis (in India, for example, where music is understood as divine and eternal, and is widely practiced in ritual), is purely practical in the Sardinian launeddas. Were it not for the circular breathing, the player would have to interrupt the drone to breathe, and this, presumably, would ruin the effect.

Though relatively obscure, the launeddas is of interest to musicologists because its form is reminiscent of the ancient Greek aulos (**12**).

210  Wolfgang Amadeus Mozart (1756–91).

211 Swing/jazz clarinetist, Benny Goodman (1909–86).

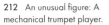

212 An unusual figure: A mechanical trumpet player.

## Clarinet music

The clarinet, which is at home in many different styles of music, has a correspondingly broad repertoire. When it was limited only to its lower (chalumeau) register, the musical possibilities were rather narrow, but with Denner's invention of the speaker key and Boehm's clapper system, the modern clarinet's musical range broadened. In addition to Wolfgang Amadeus Mozart (210), who wrote two magnificent concertos and a quintet for this instrument, romantic-era composers were particularly attracted to the clarinet. In the span of just one year, Carl Maria von Weber wrote two clarinet concertos and a concertino and Johannes Brahms wrote two sonatas with piano accompaniment and a sublime clarinet quintet.

In the 20th century, interest in the clarinet persisted and grew. Claude Debussy composed a rhapsody for clarinet. George Gershwin's *Rhapsody in Blue* opens with a famous clarinet glissando that slides into a langorous bluesy melody. Some 20th-century art composers took a fancy to wind instruments; Paul Hindemith, for example, who enriched the repertoire with a clarinet concerto and chamber music. Karlheinz Stockhausen, Helmut Lachenmann, and Wolfgang Rihm also wrote pieces for clarinet.

In jazz, clarinet and saxophone music is very much associated with certain great interpreters and improvisers. Benny Goodman (211) is the shining star of the early Swing repertoire, while Glenn Miller's typical "big band" sound offered a blending of clarinets and saxophones. To the fan, the style of a jazz musician bears a performer's signature: the sound of the saxophone

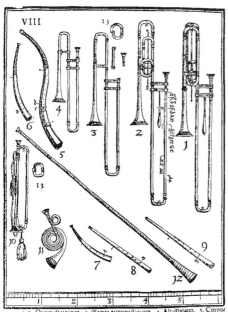

1. 2. Quart-Posaunen. 3. Rechte gemeine Posaun. 4. Alt-Posaun. 5. Corno/ Groß Tenor-Cornet. 6. Recht ChorZinck. 7. Klein DiscantZinck / so ein Quint höher. 8. Gerader Zinck mit ein Mundstück. 9. StillZinck. 10. Trommet. 11. Jäger Trommet. 12. Heßgern Trommet. 13. Krumbbügel auff ein gantz Thon.

of the great Charlie Parker is still distinctive after 40 years.

## Cups not reeds—Trumpets

A common feature of all trumpets is that they allow the musician to produce a tone by blowing through pursed lips pressed against a cup-shaped mouthpiece, so making the air inside the instrument vibrate. A further, though secondary, feature is that they are made from metal and so are grouped together under the general heading of "brass instruments" (**213**). These include trumpets, French horns, trombones, cornets, and tubas.

## Acoustical properties

Any tube that is blown into with tense lips is a trumpet instrument. Historically, this tube is

**214** A crumhorn. This instrument was already widely in use in baroque times and often played the leading voices in ensembles. The crumhorn has a soft but pronounced tone.

Wind Instruments

215   A trumpet.

coiled one or more times and ends in a horn, or "bell," which amplifies the sound. This basic instrument produces only a fundamental pitch and its natural overtones which made it useful as a signal instrument. (The notes of bugle calls such as "Reveille" and "Taps" employ these basic pitches of the overtone series.) Through overblowing, an accomplished trumpeter can produce melodies. This style of playing made the first musically meaningful application of the trumpet possible and is enormously complicated. With the addition of small finger holes, the natural overtone series of different fundamental notes can be produced, thus expanding the number of available pitches.

### Keys, slides, and valves

Like many other wind instruments, the trumpets (215) have also been mechanized. The system of keys and valves, however, is not designed for precise intonation but for steering the completely elementary acoustic processes toward the production of the natural overtone series. Unlike finger holes, which determine the pitch of a tone, the keys and valves determine which fundamental pitch will be the basis of the overtones.

   The order of three valves found on modern trumpets and horns makes the entire spectrum of chromatic pitches possible (meaning the 12 pitches of the western diatonic pitch system: C, C#, D, D#, E, F, F#, G, G#, A, A#, B). The air column is very long, since it is conducted through a complex system of coils and branches. The valves are positioned at the branches of the coils and either block them or open them, and regulate the airstream within

216   Well-known jazz trumpet player Louis "Satchmo" Armstrong (1900–71).

the instrument so that the air travels through different curves of the pipe. Acoustically, therefore, nothing happens except that the length of the vibrating air column changes, and this is what determines the pitch.

One can also change the length of the air column by making part of the pipe movable: This is the basis of the slide mechanism of the trombones (**221**).

217  As symbols of power, kettledrums and trumpets were often adorned with coats of arms.

## Kettledrums and trumpets

Trumpets have always been of interest to musicologists and historians. Their gleaming appearance and their loud tone makes them suitable for purposes that have nothing to do with their musical possibilities. Trumpets have served throughout history as a symbol of power, and trumpeters have enjoyed respect. In the 16th century, it was considered a privilege that trumpets could be played only by specially educated trumpeters in service to a court or church. The trumpeters' duties also included playing the kettledrums, which have also been a musical expression of power and dignity (**217**).

The social function of trumpets has changed in proportion to changes in social history. Of the trumpeter's privileges, nothing remains—unless one considers, perhaps, the star status sometimes conferred on trumpet players a vestige of their earlier prestige (**216**).

## The horn

Horns are frequently associated with extra-musical events. For example, the post horn and the hunting horn (**218**) were both used as practical signals—the former to announce the arrival of the mail coach in European towns, the latter for obvious purposes. Historically, horns transmitted different messages. Even if post

218  A typical hunting horn.

219 By removing pieces of pipe, one can change the pitch of the fundamental tone of this "invention horn."

220 The "flugelhorn," a variation of the trumpet, has sometimes been called a bugle.

horns and military trumpets are obsolete, the horn still fills a certain niche. The encoded information of the hunting horn, which anyone can hear but not everyone can decipher, and the players of huge alpenhorns originally designed to convey news, not to amuse tourists, suggest something of the primary function of the horn.

The French horn, however, has been a member of the orchestra since the 18th century, though it is still associated with the hunt. It is characterized by its round form and large bell. The French horn has a softer and more flexible tone than other brass instruments, and it is generally more difficult to play.

### The trombone

Trombones were already established in the music of the Middle Ages and the Renaissance. Their fundamental features—the oblong form and the slide—have not changed, though their size and tube diameter have.

The slide, which moves freely in and out, offers its own special capabilities: Minor shifts below or above the position required for a specific pitch allow the trombone player to produce abundant tonal nuances—a quality exploited by jazz players in their improvisations (**221**).

### Music for the brass instruments

The sharply contoured trumpet, the softer horn, and the flexibly toned trombone have no common repertoire, except when they have to blare out hymns in "brass choirs."

221 The slide trombone.

The trumpet repertoire consists predominantly of solo concerti composed especially during the baroque era. Composers of later generations have written only sporadically for this instrument. The relative paucity of material means that one tends to hear the same pieces over and over in the concert hall. On the other hand, many virtuoso players have transcribed compositions for other instruments and turned them into trumpet concerti to great effect. One of the earliest great works for the trumpet is the trumpet concerto of Joseph Haydn.

In the romantic-era orchestra, the trumpet had a leading part, reinforced by trombones and horns. In the symphonies of Anton Bruckner (**223**), in particular, the brass instruments have a leading role.

Less of an independent repertoire has been written for the trombone than for the trumpet. While baroque music rarely uses trombone, in the classical and romantic orchestra, it plays a role equal to the trumpet—as part of the brass section. Perhaps one of the most famous trombone solos comes in Mozart's *Requiem*, when the bass vocal soloist and trombone perform a polyphonic duet. Another famous Mozartian trombone burst occurs in the last act of *Don Giovanni*, signaling the entrance of the statue of the dead commendatore who sends the errant don to his fiery doom.

The horn, on the other hand, has historically met with considerably more regard: Mozart, Brahms, and Richard Strauss all composed music for the horn.

**222**  Medieval book illumination of a trumpeter and a drummer.

**223**  Anton Bruckner (1824–96).

Wind Instruments

**224** A serpent—a large cornet in the form of a snake.

## Individuality and extravagance

Music cannot be grasped as an object. It is not like a painting or a drawing or a sculpture. It exists only in performance and the sound experience is unique. It is true that it can be recorded, and in this way duplicated, but the unique experience of the live performance eludes efforts at preservation anywhere but in the memory of the participants. When musical instruments are used in the performance of a composition or in free improvisations, they directly determine the resulting sound and are an essential part of the music itself. If one has the chance to watch or listen in on a rehearsal, it becomes clear that the substance of the composition remains unchanged but the piece may assume a wholly other tonal character. Phrasing and emphasis, accents and dynamics take on different weights. The treatment of the music thus gives the piece a second musical and aesthetic existence. The form and arrangement of an interpretation of a musical work very much depend on taste and fashion.

## Oddities

The desire for originality, or in its darker incarnation notoriety, is not unique to our own time. Instrument makers in every era have taken it upon themselves to produce unusual and sometimes bizarre sound-producing apparatuses whose form, sound, and operation do not derive from musical or aesthetic needs. By this definition, the giraffe piano (**35**) is a bizarre instrument indeed.

**225** A rankett.

## Changing functions

Instruments may be considered unusual when they are musically usable only under certain circumstances or exist only to produce special effects. By this standard, which may not be an altogether fair standard, the saxophone, originally developed for military bands and eventually a staple of jazz, would be a highly unusual instrument to find in a symphony orchestra.

## Special forms

In addition to clearly odd instruments and those that are unusual in a certain musical context, there are instruments that appear bizarre in form but whose construction is based on musically acoustical grounds. The rankett (**225**), a double-reed instrument with the extremely descriptive name of *Wurstfagott* ("sausage bassoon"), contains a multiply-wound air column that enables a much deeper tone to be produced than might be expected from such a small instrument (it is only 5 to 10 inches long). Like the rankett, which was invented approximately between 1550 and 1651, a number of other instruments in the history of music have remained ever on the fringe.

## The marine trumpet

Medieval illustrations often depict a string instrument with a

**226** The marine trumpet, or monochord.

particularly striking form. The marine trumpet was widespread until the early 17th century when it vanished. The German name *Trumscheit* is derived from *trumme*, denoting either a trumpet tube or drum, and *scheit*, meaning a piece of wood. In fact, the name is not as arbitrary as it sounds since the marine trumpet actually produces a droning tone due to its construction. Only a single string is drawn over the bridge, which is itself moveable and strikes periodically against the top of the instrument as it is played. The instrument was also known as the "trumpet fiddle," the "nun fiddle," or the "tromba marina," but the

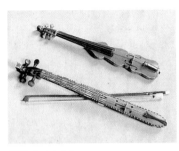

227   Pocket violins.

latter two terms are inexplicable since the instrument had nothing to do with either convents or the sea.

### Deviations from the norm

Any deviation from what one is used to seeing is likely to appear unusual. Musical instruments are no exception. Miniature instruments are often underrated as nonfunctional objects that may, at best, be useful for demonstration purposes. This has by no means always been the case. The conspicuously small form of the so-called dancemaster fiddles, or pocket or kit violins (**227**), was eminently practical. The dancemaster, who had to supply the music and direct his pupils' steps simultaneously, could do this best with a small and handy instrument. Because of its very narrow soundbox, the tone of the violin is rather less beautiful than piercing—an advantage for the master whose pedagogical purposes would not have

been served by a quieter instrument.

### Mixed forms

Some instruments are unusual combinations of the forms and mechanisms of other instruments. Such instruments generally only enjoy a short lifespan.

One example is the arpeggione, a cross between a cello and a guitar. The only reason this instrument is still known today is that Franz Schubert composed a sonata for it. Another example is the baryton, which is related to the gamba family but has an additional row of strings (aliquot

228   "Stick" violins.

strings) that are plucked with the left thumb. Technical mastery of the instrument is extremely difficult. The baryton was the preferred instrument of Prince Nicolas Esterházy, the patron of Joseph Haydn, who composed 175 works for the unusual instrument. In contrast to the arpeggione sonata, which is today played on the cello or the viola and counts among the standard works in their repertoire, Haydn's baryton works are almost never played.

In addition to the arpeggione and baryton and their ilk, which are combinations of two string instruments, instrument makers have sometimes united two completely different kinds of instruments. A spinettregal (229), for example, is a small organ and a plucked string instrument; its use is extremely limited. It might best be regarded as an experiment of no practical use.

The external form of an instrument is of course no indication of its uniqueness or oddity. Both the form and structural characteristics of various instruments have developed and changed in the course of history. The preservation or modification of forms has not always been driven by the quest for better acoustical quality or new properties, but is often just a matter of aesthetic preference. For most instruments, listeners simply take modifications in stride. Variations among string instruments— such as changes in the shape of the soundboxes—are so common as to be unnoteworthy.

The same is true for drums and other percussion instruments. Wind

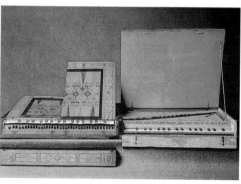

229   Two people can play while a third provides the air.

instruments, on the other hand, are generally expected to look and act the same. They are pipes; they are either straight or wound; they may be blown lengthwise or transversely. The ocarina (230), which is a flute, defies this insistence on the status quo of wind instruments. It is oval—originally probably egg-shaped; the many ethnic ocarinas from around the world occur in a variety of shapes, from animals to multifaced creatures. The body and mouth

are set sideways. The name in Italian means "little goose."
With up to 8 or 10 fingerholes distributed irregularly around the body of the instrument, here, too, the ocarina breaks the rules.

### Imitations of sounds

To design an instrument with as versatile and colorful a tone as possible is the goal of the instrument maker. The various registers of an organ or a harpsichord exemplify this drive. There are no limits on the imaginations of the instrument makers, who have always been known for experimenting with an enormous range of materials—using alloys for organ pipes and harpsichord strings, small bits of leather in place of the

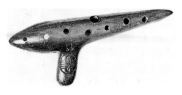

230 An ocarina.

traditional quill, using electronic circuits instead of resonators, using a steel body on a guitar, or a plucking mechanism on a lute. Necessity is not always the mother of invention: Sometimes invention is born of a simple human urge called creativity. And the results are only considered "bizarre" or "unusual" to the extent that they did or did not catch on. Electric

pianos, synthesizers, pedal steel guitars, string benders for changing tuning—all transcend the field of the idle experiment by their widespread adoption, albeit not in the symphony milieu.

Some early instrument makers sought innovation in techniques that altered the tone of an instrument and radically changed its sound. Flemish virginals contain a mechanism that pushes a small metal hook against the string. This "arpichordium" emits a whirring sound quite unlike the original signature sound of the virginal. The piano has not escaped efforts to expand its sound possibilities, even on the concert grand. The "Janissary device," popular in the early 19th century, combines several processes to change the basic sound of the instrument. A curved metal bar struck against the lower strings created a cymbal-like clang, while a metal pin caused several bells to sound at the same time. The device was further enriched by a pedal mechanism that struck against the back side of the sound board with a leather mallet to resemble a drum. The name of the innovation comes from Janissary music, a Turkish percussion ensemble that became popular, with the short life of most fads, in Europe at the end of the 18th century. Many European composers wrote under the influence of the Janissary style,

# Bizarre and Unusual Instruments

including Mozart in his *Piano Sonata in A Minor* (KV 331).

## Preparations

It was not the imitation of another sound but the structural alteration of the existing sound that John Cage had in mind when he began to "prepare" the traditional piano. By clamping ordinary household articles such as spoons, nails, or erasers between the piano's strings, for example, Cage intervened directly in the process of tone production. In so doing, he raised serious questions about the whole process of tone production on the piano and about aesthetics. This prepared piano is anything but a bizarre instrument, although it remains unquestionably unusual.

## Mechanization

The increasing mechanization that improved the intonation of wind instruments and allowed them to attain certain tonal registers has been an undisputable advance for flutes, clarinets, and oboes. How

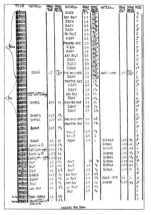

231 A page of a "prepared piano" score by John Cage.

much of a boon mechanization implied for other classes of instruments is less clear. While the mechanics of the piano have become ever more complicated, the production of the tone itself—the striking of the hammer—has remained unchanged. Mechanization taken to an extreme may be technically impressive, but its natural end product, automation, may be anything but an improvement in the history of music. The piano roll used for the player piano controls the duration and dynamics of the hammer strokes of the piece of music, making the piece reproduceable at will. On the other hand, the piece is inflexible; it cannot vary, and the player piano cannot be played with any personal affect, or in an ensemble,

232 John Cage's prepared piano.

**233** This gramophone horn broadcasts sound especially well.

**234** Musical clocks use perforated metal plates as a storage mechanism.

unless musicians are willing to be led by a recorded performance. Still, the piano rolls offer one valuable possibility: Many were recorded by the original composers or by past virtuoso pianists, and so they capture a bit of musical history in their own way.

## Reproduction at the push of a button

A gramophone is not a true instrument in neither the scientific sense nor in popular understanding. Likewise, the small so-called musical clocks (**234**), in which a metal pin on a roller lifts and sets a small metal tongue vibrating, is not an instrument, unless (at a stretch) one classifies it as an idiophone. Such devices do nothing more than reproduce acoustical signals.

Their successors, however, may well be the only means by which millions of people come in contact with music—namely, electronically.

## One of a kind
Every so often an invention comes down the pike that never catches on, and as such may be called "bizarre and unusual," though in principle or theory, it has a deep and lasting impact on the world. Such an instrument

**235** Sound recording ca. 1890.

**236** This strangely shaped gramophone horn only partially serves its purpose.

is the Theremin, named for its Russian inventor, Lev Termen, who brought it to New York in the early part of the 20th century. The Theremin is an electronic instrument that operates on the principle of heterodyning two radio frequency oscillators. The player moves her hands (the feminine pronoun is quite deliberate here since the world's greatest Theremin player was a woman) to and fro in midair before two antennae, one of which controls the pitch, the other the volume. The closer the hand to the respective antennae, the higher the pitch or the louder the sound. At the hands (literally) of a virtuoso, the instrument could attain remarkable nuance of intonation and musicality.

Today, the somewhat eerie, wobbly sound of the Theremin may only be heard on soundtracks for 1950s horror movies or camped-up television commercials, or on many early rock n' roll tracks. A documentary video on the instrument and its mysterious inventor shows the Theremin, Terman, and his small following in action. But this bizarre instrument influenced future generations, from Robert Moog (who would patent the first electronic synthesizer) to Brian Wilson of the Beach Boys, and may be legitimately considered the forerunner of modern electronic music.

**237** Thomas Alva Edison, the inventor of the phonograph, used wax rolls to record and play back sound.

## Musical beat-keepers

It doesn't take much to set one's fingers tapping—on a table, on one's knee, out of nervousness, in a rhythm, out of step. The drumming impulse may well be a non-verbal effort to communicate, and as elemental a part of human existence as the first vocalizations of a newborn baby. All it takes is some minor direction from the conscious mind to turn what is often unconscious into an ordered pattern of sounds that might well be called music.

The first string instruments were hunting bows strung with animal sinews; the first wind instruments were flutes made of reed and bone. The makings of early drums were equally available: Animal skins and pelts were ordinary materials. Obviously though, as skins per se they were fairly useless as musical instruments. Not too many people make the beating of a rug into music. To produce an audible, practical, and variable sound, they need to be altered. Like the strings of the musical bow, hides also had to be stretched in order to make a vibrating surface (      ).

Among all the components of what we think of as music, the key to creating sound through vibrating membranes, or skins, is rhythm. No other single class of instruments is bound quite so closely to a single musical parameter. This is not to say that drums cannot also be used in varying pitches, but certainly their role in sustaining or creating rhythmic patterns is most consistent with the common perception of the drum. In terms of their origin and history, we can find depictions of drums in ancient rock paintings; such evidence is normally interpreted as a sign of their ritual and communicative function in

**238** Ancient rock paintings showing a drum and a musical bow.

Drums

"pre-music," as it were.

In the music of many non-western cultures, drums with stretched heads (called membrano-phones, from the Greek *membrana*, for skin, and *phonein*, for sound) have such an important function that it is hard to imagine such music without them. Turkish, Arabian, and Indian music, for example, is extremely complex in its rhythmic structure. In these as well as many other cultures and subcultures, the structure of the rhythm is just as important as the development of the melody. It is not surprising that various kinds of drums and drumming techniques are highly valued in Arabic and Indian culture (see p. 142).

239  Native American drummer simultaneously playing a flute. The person standing wears rattles on his ankles and plays a clapper.

In African music, the drum is not the only vehicle for carrying the rhythmic element. Through many-layered superimpositions of rhythmical patterns, a dominant sound is established while the melodic element continues as background. The various membranophones found in African cultures are often beautifully made and well-crafted, reflecting their special standing as instruments and as tribal art.

Western musical culture takes a somewhat different approach to the drum. In so-called serious music, they are used specifically in orchestras, usually as background instruments. In most streams of jazz, pop, and rock n' roll, on the other

Drums

240 Modern orchestral kettledrums (timpani) are tuned by a pedal mechanism.

hand, they are a prevalent and obvious part of the sound.

### A skin stretched over a kettle— The timpanum

The unique role of the timpanun, or kettledrum (    ), in the history of European music is not generally appreciated. Along with trumpets, it was an instrument of authority used to express, through music, the power and influence of a sovereign.

Like many instruments, the kettledrum came to Europe from the Arabic world. Since the time of the crusades in the 11th through the 13th centuries, it was primarily used for military music (    ).

### Construction

The heads (vibrating membranes) of the kettledrum are stretched over a kettle-shaped resonating chamber. This slim description of its external features in itself distinguishes these membranophones from other drums. By the time of the Renaissance, the upper edge of the "kettle" was fitted with a screw mechanism by which the head could be tightened or loosened to vary the instrument's pitch. This mechanism was used exclusively until 1837, when a pedal mechanism was

241 Music was often used in the Middle Ages and Renaissance to demonstrate power and prestige. Kettledrums were frequently used this way.

attached to allow the timpanist to tune to a different pitch much faster. Some percussionists, however, still prefer the tone of hand-tuned drums. Modern orchestras usually include three to five timpani.

**Playing technique**

Kettledrums are played with mallets, consisting of sticks whose heads may be covered with felt, flannel, wood, or foam rubber. The different mallet heads produce different qualities of tone—the softer material produces a softer tone. The player may also change the tone by using a mute (*coperto*) or a cloth, or by placing his or her palm on the drum head. As a rule, the player strikes the head about a hand's breadth away from the edge. The point of impact determines the tonal character. Near the edge, the tone is full and complex, rich in overtones, while it becomes duller as the drum is struck nearer its center.

Kettledrums are usually tuned to the tonic (key note) and dominant (5th tone of the scale) of the key of the piece being played. If the piece has no clear key, as is the case in some 20th-century music, the drums are tuned according to the composer's instructions.

Among drumming techniques, the drumroll—the specialty of all drums sounded with sticks or mallets—is also a quintessential element in timpani playing. This sequence of rapid blows on the drum head usually starts softly and increases in volume. Composers

242 The Janissaries of Turkey also knew the symbolic power of the kettledrum.

Drums

often use drumrolls from the timpani to dramatic effect in a musical climax, where their deep, powerful vibration has a strong effect on the listener.

## Two heads are better than one?
## The drum

While "drum" is used as an umbrella term for all membranophones—much as "lute" encompasses an array of plucked string instruments—the word also has a more narrow application. It describes an instrument that has a cylindrical resonator with a drum head (stretched membrane) on either end, though usually only one side is played.

The two-headed drum never attained the stature of the kettledrum in symphonic and so-called serious music. Such drums were preferred for marching music, a considerably more limited repertoire. But outside the symphony hall, drummers enjoy a vast popular appeal. They have always appeared in bands at fairs and festivals, often dressed in folkloric costumes, in many ways as a vestige of old, traditional musical customs which retain traces of the evocative power of drumming.

As orchestral instruments, several sizes of drums are used. The drums are not tuned to a specific pitch but have standardized voices according to their size and construction. The largest is the bass drum, which, as its name suggests, produces a low, thunderous tone.

**243** Different types of drums from *Syntagma musicum* (1615–19) by Michael Praetorius.

Drums

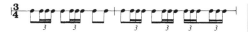

**244** This drum rhythm continues all the way through the famous *Bolero* of Maurice Ravel.

While only some orchestras use the mid-sized tenor drum, the snare drum, or side drum, is a staple of percussion sections. Across its bottom membrane, the snare drum has a set of strings, or snares, that vibrate when the top membrane is struck. This produces a rattling tone that adds tremendously to the drum's carrying power and dramatic effect. With a few exceptions (    ), the two-sided drums still take a back seat to the kettledrums in western "classical" music, although, as always in the dynamic nature of musical development, the snare has come into its own with Igor Stravinsky and 20th-century orchestration.

As is true of the entire nomenclature of musical instruments, the range of terminology having to do wth drums is large and somewhat tangled. For large drums, the Italian *gran cassa* and the French *grosse caisse* are one and the same. But, is the *caisse claire* always a snare drum or could it possibly be the French *tambour*, a small drum used in the folk music of Provence?

Illustrations and descriptions of membranophones of every form and construction appear in esoteric books of the Renaissance and the baroque period (    ). These certainly confirm the continuing popularity of kettledrums, and of other drums as well. They have, moreover, always served as dance accompaniment,

**245** The parade of hunters marching through a peasant church festival is led by a drummer. Painting by Pieter Brueghel after Pieter Balten.

Drums

**246** Drums and castanets are often held high above the head for playing and for appearances.

marking the rhythm and keeping the tempo. And this tradition has changed little—except that dance music is less a component of the symphony or aristocratic ball and more a part of pop culture, in discos, at weddings, and at rock concerts where fans may be seen dancing in the aisles.

### "Hey, Mr. Tambourine Man!"

Linguistically, "tambourine" is a diminutive of tambour, a small French drum. The tambourine's membrane, however, is stretched over a shallow wooden hoop rather than a cylinder. Set inside the hoop-shaped frame are pairs of small circular metal plates that ring or jingle when the tambourine is struck or shaken.

The tambourine is common throughout the Mediterannean region. It is held with one hand and struck with the other (     ). The designation *tabl*, *tabir*, or *tabil* originates from an Arabic-Persian source and includes other drum instruments. Also, in Arabic and Indian cultures, the technique of playing drums with the hands is more common than playing with mallets. Thus, two different features of the tambourine—its etymology and its playing technique—suggest its origin in Arabic culture, though there is also evidence that instruments of identical form were used in ancient Rome.

### Drums in Arabic and Indian music

In Arabic and Indian music, rhythm is at least as important as melody. Percussion instruments structure the entire metrical-rhythmic course of this music. The structure of Arabic as well as Indian music rests on a comparatively simple foundation, which in execution, however, leads to a highly artistic and complex musical form.

**247** Basque one-handed drum with flute. This combination of instruments is common in the Pays basque region of the south of France and northern Spain.

Drums

The individual notes of a melody line are developed according to rigid rules, are ornamented, and form the basis for improvised elaborations, which may be played or sung. The drum lays down a pattern of complex rhythms that proceed in a peaceful, multidimensional meter and are repeated constantly. When a specific metric-rhythmic cycle is completed, the soloist proceeds to the next melodic note and improvises on it. When the player reaches the final tone of the melodic pattern (or scale), he or she returns to the first note and thus closes the cycle. The musician has some discretion regarding how often a metric cycle should be repeated before passing on to the next note. For this reason, pieces of music built around this compositional scheme vary in length. In Arabic music, the melodic model and its elaboration are called maqam, in Indian music, raga.

The drums that accompany the solo instrument or voice in Arabic and Indian music are very different from one another. The Arabic darabukka is a cup-shaped drum that is held under the left arm and played with the right hand. North Indian music uses a pair of drums, the tabla and the bayan (     ), played on the floor and in the lap. In southern India, musicians play the mrdangam, a drum with two membranes that are both struck.

The circular image, which is found so frequently in Indian philosophy, is very particularly reflected in Indian music. In this culture, the instrument that is such an essential part of the transformation of thought into acoustic form enjoys a status in proportion to its musical/spiritual role. Players are highly respected.

**248** Bayan and tabla, northern Indian paired drums.

Drums

**249** Drumming in African and Asian cultures has a ritualistic purpose. Its musicality is a secondary concern, though not to those who bring the music to Africa's urban centers and expand upon its tribalistic roots.

## Drums for incantation

In the musical cultures of eastern Asia, which vary among themselves but all trace their origins back to Chinese sources, drums serve different functions. Traditionally, drumming has been associated with magic effects. The use of drums as ritual instruments means that they may not be played by just anyone at any time, but only by designated people on certain occasions (     ). The act of communicating with the spiritual world was officially reserved for a few persons of a particular psychic bent who felt a calling. Such shamans mediated between the human and the supernatural world. Beside such emblems of social rank as elaborate headdresses and clothing, drums are a particular token of the shaman. Many shamanic cultures—as well as some putatively developed ones (in the 19th century, séances were all the rage in some circles in Europe and America)—hold that spirits can possess certain objects. The shaman's "spirit drum" was a voice through which the spirits could communicate with the earthly world. Examples of spirit drums are common in Native American, Siberian, and Himalayan cultures—the former quite likely related via migrations across the land bridge from Asia.

## Barrels and hourglasses

There are at least as many different shapes and forms of membrano-phones in the countries of eastern Asian as there are in the African cultures most often associated with drum traditions.

**250** The Japanese otsuzumi. The pitch of this drum can be changed by tightening the cords.

In the traditional music of Japan, some drums are played in ensembles organized like monastic communities where the members dedicate themselves to learning and perfecting their drumming. The odaiko (Japanese for "large drum") is played with huge mallets and requires a great deal of both physical exertion and mental concentration.

**251** An otsuzumi player.

The traditional Japanese No theater uses an hourglass-shaped  drum called an otsu-zumi (     ) that has membranes on either end. The external form of the otsuzumi also affects its acoustic qualities and playing technique. Ropes are drawn between the two heads on the drum's outside. The player holds the instrument under one arm and compresses the ropes with the other hand, thereby changing the tension on the drum heads and their pitch and tone. The player beats the

Drums

drum with only the middle finger of the right hand (    ).

The concentration necessary to play any musical instrument is nowhere more evident than in a performance of Japanese music. Like Indian music, traditional Japanese music also reflects the central philosophy, in this case derived from Buddhism, that solidity and stability are illusions and everything is in a state of continuous change.

**252** Hollow tree trunks make excellent percussion instruments.

## The drum, the instrument of Africa

The stereotypical image of Africans ever drumming often prevails over the fact that Africa has many other indigenous instruments and that drumming itself is capable of highly differentiated and complex musical expression.

African drums come in all shapes and types (    ). They are often accompanied by other instruments and other drums, and, by overlaying different melodic or rhythmic structures, the ensemble can produce an entirely new musical whole. The whole, of course, is greater than the sum of the parts. For example, two drummers simultaneously play different rhythms; the listener, however, does not necessarily perceive the rhythm as coming from two instruments but hears a single musical sound. These complementary intervals and rhythms are composed of repeated patterns or forms.

Drumming with variable pitch also is common in some African cultures. The drums use a cord mechanism like that of the Japanese otsuzumi. This capability of producing change-able pitches on a single drum makes such instruments suited for transmission of differentiated information. Many African languages vary word meanings by varying the pitch pattern of otherwise identical words or phrases, much as the change in rhythmic stress from one syllable to another may change the meaning of a word in Russian and other Slavic languages. The variable pitch of certain African drums, thus, allows them to emulate human speech more effectively.

253  Corded-drum player.

## Hollow logs with sound holes

Hollowed-out tree trunks can make marvelous percussion instruments; all they need is an opening through which the sound can escape. Instruments based on this simple acoustic mechanism are called slotted drums; they come in many sizes and can be quite simple or complex. When struck with large sticks, these vibrating logs can make a very loud sound—again, an advantage in old-fashioned long-distance communication. (Technically, the designation "drum" is inappropriate for these instruments—they should be more strictly classified as idiophones (see pp. 160 ff.) African drums of all kinds have found their way into western music, if not yet into the

254  These cup-shaped drums from Zaire are played with both sticks and hands.

147

**255** The classic drum set.

western symphonic repertoire. The emergence of African drums is seen in the folk music revival of this century and derived, of course, through the forced migrations of African peoples through the slave trade as well as the emigration of Africans to the countries of Europe and North America.

**Percussion: Drums in western music**

Drums, or membranophones, are central to musical practice in most cultures, although this is not always true in Europe and North America. Before the 20th century, percussion instruments played a marginal role in classical music. In those styles of music meant to accompany and facilitate movement, for example military marches and dances, percussion becomes considerably more important. John Phillip Sousa (1854–1932), renowned bandmaster and march composer whose music has stirred and symbolized American patriotism, said, "a march should make a man with a wooden leg step out."

One realm of western music in which the role of drums is undisputed is jazz, rock, and pop. This is not surprising if one considers the historical roots of these musical styles: jazz is generally considered an outgrowth of African-American musical traditions, as, for that matter, is rock and roll. The instrumentation of jazz was also influenced by military bands.

The standard percussion instruments for jazz, rock and pop are contained in the "drum set"— the configuration that became stamped on many a baby boomer's mind with "The Beatles" printed across the front skin of the bass drum— which can be expanded to achieve, for example, a bigger sound, as in "hard rock." A basic drum set (**255**) includes the bass drum, played with a foot pedal, the snare, and two different-sized tom-toms. One of these is free-standing, the other fastened to the bass drum. The typical drum sets also has sets of cymbals, which may be played with a pedal causing them to clap against each other (hi-hats) or they may be hit with drumsticks or with brushes for a softer sound. (Technically, the cymbals are idiophones.) Of the drums in the typical drum set, the bass and the snare drums have no exactly fixed pitches; tom-toms, however, may.

In jazz, rock, and pop groups the drums keep the musicians on the beat—usually four-four, but sometimes three-four time. And while the drummer keeps the ensemble together, the drum sound may be subtle or dominant; there is plenty of latitude for syncopation and individual style. Jazz and rock have in fact become showcases for drummers, who often get to perform solos and can attract a great following.

### Music for percussion instruments

Very few pieces specifically for percussion instruments are included in the baroque, classical, or romantic repertoire of western concert halls. While Joseph Haydn's "Paukenschlag [Drumbeat] Symphony" does not directly belong in this canon, it is of interest as a curiosity. Percussion works did not really appear in the serious orchestra hall until the 20th century, when Béla Bartòk composed his *Music for String Instruments, Percussion and Celesta* and *Sonata for Two Pianos and Percussion*. From the minimalist composers, one piece scored only for percussion has become famous: *Drumming* by Steve Reich (**256**). We must also mention the great young Scottish percussion virtuosa Evelyn Glennie, who tours the world giving concerts and commissions pieces from well-known composers. She also happens to be deaf.

256   Steve Reich (*1936).

Drums

**257** In the Middle Ages, the relationship between music and religion was especially close. This section from the Isenheim Altar by Matthias Grünewald portays an angel playing a gamba. There were no doubt artistic reasons for the artist to depict the angel in this peculiar playing position.

## The mirror of musical culture

Musical instruments are a tangible expression of the cultural and aesthetic self-image of a society or a group within the society. Almost every instrument fulfills functions that are unrelated to music and extend far beyond its role as a sound-producing apparatus.

## Devices for sound and ritual

Evidence exists that various ancient cultures used musical instruments as ritual paraphernalia. In many cases, the use of the devices was limited to certain persons or groups who acted as priests in the fulfillment of ritual religious services.

Already in the 3rd millennium BC, the close relationship between musical and cult devices began to relax. In Mesopotamia, for example, it is possible to trace differences between sacred and profane music, each of which used instruments appropriate to its needs.

In addition to music performed by the priests as an integral part of the religious ritual service, professional musicians played other music at feasts and holidays and similar occasions. In ancient Greece, the shrill tone of the aulos made the instrument unpopular in ritual service, but later it became quite common.

## Professional musicians and virtuosi

The social opinion of a musical instrument often depends on who plays it and for what purpose. Virtuoso aulos players who earned money from their skill were denigrated for practicing a mere craft and lacking spirit. In fact, many a technical wizard has been criticized for lacking spirit in his or her playing; it is just somewhat startling to hear the same old saw from ancient Greece. In the 19th century, this complaint was rampant when mas-

# The Social and Cultural Context of Instruments

**258** In ancient Greece, the lyre was used pedagogically in the education of free citizens; it also served as accompaniment for singers and poets—could Homer have been accompanied by a lyre?

ter pianists performed repertoires of great difficulty, but questionable musicality, on concert stages.

## Social hierarchy

The social significance of instruments through the course of history often has had less to do with their specific instrumental properties—such as relative ease or difficulty in playing or the range of sounds and pitches the instrument is capable of producing—than with some arbitrary and irrational social trend or fashion. To speak of a "queen of instruments" or a poor man's bass fiddle (a washtub bass) is of more interest in social history than in acoustic history. That, in the western world, the symphony orchestra is looked upon as the domain of the wealthy, while a street musician fiddles away for spare change and is looked upon as one small step above a derelict again says more about our social mores than our musical tastes. The street musician, in the course of his or her

career, may well entertain more individuals than a first cello in the Boston Symphony Orchestra. But the latter will invariably enjoy more remuneration and more prestige, and the instrument itself may assume a higher social rank in this artificial hierarchy of instruments.

It defies explanation why the olifant, a carved ivory horn, was seen as a symbol of knightly power, or why the crwth, a stringed instrument simultaneously bowed and plucked, was revered as the instrument of the Celtic bards. These values are a matter of historical record, though they remain fairly inexplicable.

The origin of the social standing of instruments such as the harp, the bass drum, and the trumpet, on the other hand, seems at least understandable, if not necessarily justifiable. For thousands of years, the harp

**259** Music was a component of medieval revels.

has been associated with the biblical King David and with angels. It is no wonder, then, that it is thought of as a mark of the delicate, the spiritual, and as a ladies' instrument.

From the Middle Ages to the baroque period, kettle and bass drums and trumpets were the emblems of power. While this peculiar signification is obsolete today, their image—to say nothing of their sound or application—is evocative of baroque brilliance and festivity, a fact not lost upon the marketing directors of the music recording industry. If they were primarily thought of as military instruments, they might enjoy a quite different reputation. What exactly that would be is hard to say. What, after all, is the reputation of the fife and drum? Ambivalent at best.

## Social connections—
## It's not what you know ...

In the clearly defined class structure of medieval society, certain instruments were exclusively associated

with specific social groups. We have already considered the "nobility" of the harp, the martial authority of the kettledrum and the trumpet. These were the aristocrats of instruments. There was also a great underclass. The hurdy-gurdy, for example (18), was at one time the instrument of beggars; it is also a good example of how some instruments experienced upward social mobility as they became first a curiosity or novelty, then a collectible, then instruments of the bourgeoisie, and finally an eclectic hallmark of the aristocrat.

The change in status often grows out of a change in philosophy. In France, the birthplace of the Enlightenment, a new interest in "natural man" coupled with demands for simplicity led both the nobility and the middle class to adopt that simple instrument, the hurdy-gurdy. Although even very challenging works like Antonio Vivaldi's *Four Seasons* were arranged for the instrument, playing the hurdy-gurdy remained a passing fancy, like the pastoral drama, of the middle and upper classes.

## Stereotyped images
The hurdy-gurdy is not the only instrument to undergo a social metamorphosis, but such transformations have often passed

260   This medieval illustration depicts a queen playing a psaltery which, along with violin-like instruments, was much beloved by the nobility.

261 With instruments, unusual artistic design has always been a sign of particular taste. The player was even willing to accept that the small nuts would interfere with proper tuning of the strings.

unnoticed by the musical public. Acquaintance with the hurdy-gurdy varies from region to region, and in any case, interest in the instrument has tended to remain the province of music specialists and folk musicians. In contrast, almost everyone associates the bagpipes or the zither with Scotland and the Alps, respectively. But in fact, bagpipes are found throughout Europe, and the zither occurs in exceedingly various forms in every musical culture of the world.

## Unchanging Function

Peculiar in the history of music, one instrument has occupied basically the same social position throughout its long life—the

organ. While this constancy has secured its survival and preserved its uniqueness, it has also limited its musical opportunities. Consigned to the realm of the sacred in an increasingly secular world, played as a part of church services particularly in the rituals of Protestant and Catholic practice, the organ retains a static position.

Musically, the function of the organ has experienced very little change, least of all in its overwhelmingly predominant role of accompanying songs of praise. So entrenched is this perception of the religious voice of the organ that much organ music sounds religious in nature, even if it is not. An organ toccata originally intended to showcase the technical qualities of the instrument and the player or a fugue meant to display the composer's wealth of invention and unique mastery of compositional technique both retain something of a religious air even when they are played in concert. This is not to suggest that there are not wonderful secular

262 No instrument is so strongly associated with gypsy music as the dulcimer. Even in the 19th century, this form of dulcimer was considered typically Hungarian and associated with the music of the Sinti and Roma.

**263** French harpsichords were often ornately painted and decorated. They functioned as status symbols of the nobility and wealthy members of the bourgeoisie.

This is a curious phenomenon, for few other objects meet this fate—pottery, maybe, but in general, most tools of the arts or of trades remain just what they are: tools. No one keeps old paintbrushes on their living room wall. But musical instruments, perhaps precisely because of their special position in cultural and social history, are treasured out of context as well as in.

Collecting musical instruments is no different from collecting stamps or coins or dolls or baseball cards. Maybe the collector has an aesthetic affinity for the objects, and maybe he or she hopes they will grow in value. Maybe they represent a certain challenge—how many can one

organ pieces; it is simply to demonstrate how deeply a consistent acoustic and social history can mark our more limited imaginations, leaving us with little more than a stereotype and some rather dulled senses.

## The collector's passion

Many people who do not play music have musical instruments. Perhaps they are inherited legacies. Perhaps they are abandoned childhood pursuits. Perhaps they are oddities picked up cheaply at a flea market. Perhaps they are a fad in interior decorating. Whatever the cue that brings them into our lives, musical instruments have most clearly assumed a value as objects, with little necessary connection to their function as musical instruments.

**264** Embellishment and decoration are not unique to our own culture. The monsur, a Mongolian string instrument, lends itself to being used as a status symbol.

collect? Can one find that rare Sumerian lute? There is a certain side of collecting musical instruments, however, that cuts deeper than the passions for other collectibles. Unplayed, musical instruments lose their *raison d'être*. This may not bother the collector, just as the art collector may not care if he hoards his priceless Van Gogh painting in a vault. But the serious collector, who appreciates the nature of the objects he or she collects, will allow concert musicians to borrow the instruments on a long-term basis, and thereby allow the public access to the instruments. Even museum collections are sometimes played, though never by the public. But museum pieces may be used in special concerts. Moreover, the simple fact is that the instruments actually last better with some use, and use is the best indicator of their need for particular care.

**265** Until well into the 20th century, the printing and distribution of broadsides with songs and simple ballads were a popular means of transmitting musical culture.

## From experiment to mass effectiveness

In certain respects, as stated earlier, the continuous development within the field of musical instruments was completed in the middle of the 19th century. This is manifest today in the standardization of modern ensemble and orchestral instruments. There have been no significant changes since the last century in the configuration of the symphony orchestra. And there is apparently no need for change so long as orchestras continue to draw upon the same musical repertoire.

While some say change is inevitable, in western music it has usually been required to establish its own terms. Some contemporary-music trends have witnessed attempts to apply technical innovations for various purposes. They have had to assert themselves, for the most part, outside the larger city philharmonia—in experimental music, in those academic settings that grant free rein for innovation outside the mainstream, in jazz, rock, world music, and synthesis.

As computers and electronic media were introduced into the musical domain, revolutionizing the ideolo-

**266** The performance of a municipal orchestra is not always well received. Caricatures have always been a favorite means to poke fun at musicians and the "noise" they make.

gical underpinnings and the tonal reality of musical history, one composer plunged in as a pioneer. If for no other reason than his recognition of the significance and potential of electronic music generation, the German composer Karlheinz Stockhausen must be considered one of the most important composers of the 20th century. A successful composer originally of more conventional contemporary orchestral music, opera, chamber music, and more, Stockhausen has spent years experimenting with ways of using taped and electronically generated sound along with traditional instruments.

So far as synthesized music is concerned, electronic instruments are here to stay, if for no other reason than that they are affordable, practical, and portable. And, like computers themselves (which at some point also may well have to be considered musical instruments), they seem to have a certain attraction to some people, especially young people. It is not far-fetched to suppose that in such young people this attraction will grow, and that they will, like the preceding generations of the 20th century, explore the possibilities of these instruments until they too become traditional in their own right.

## The big-city orchestra— A mark on a map

The function of individual instruments as symbols of power has shifted in the course of history; examples of such change are plentiful. However, attitudes toward great sound mechanisms like the symphony orchestra or smaller ensembles like the chamber orchestra or the string quartet have not changed very much. Many a city council or civic authority has done cartwheels in its efforts to establish a high-quality symphony orchestra, wrestling with sources of community financing and patrons of the arts beyond the call of duty, and beyond the pale of musical reality. Those cities that have outstanding resident orchestras—not just New York but Boston, Chicago, Philadelphia, Cleveland, Miami, Denver, and more (to name only cities in the United States)— would find the idea of losing those assets (for cultural assets they are) for lack of endowments, patrons, or federal funding, unthinkable. The symphony is, in no uncertain terms, a symbol of prestige for a city.

**267** Private concerts are often festive occasions and social events. Today the idea of making music at home carries a dilettantish hue, but not so the private concert pictured here: Franz Schubert is sitting at the piano.

**268** One can easily imagine how much fun it was for these children to play their instruments. The boy on the right in the picture plays a "Rommel-pot," a vessel holding a pig bladder with a staff stuck through it. The grater produces a grunting noise. Painting by Jan Miense Molenaer.

## Self-sounding instruments

Before it occurred to early humans to beat on a stretched animal hide or blow into a reed or pluck the string of a bow, they must have noticed that all solid materials gave off a noise or even a pitch of their own when struck together, hit with a stick, or rubbed against something else. How basic this process is and how often it occurs in daily life is evidenced by small children who clap toys together or by adults who rattle their keys. In all these cases, the entire object is set vibrating. While all these instances are examples of idiophones (from the Greek *idios*, for self), they would only become musical instruments when the action that produces the sound is undertaken with some sort of music-making intention.

The idiophones planned as musical instruments vary so widely in form that all their external features cannot possibly be described here. We can, however, just for the sake of follow-through, return to Hornbostel and Sachs for a description of the overarching idiophonic classification criteria of the position and method of playing.

There are idiophones with definite and variable pitch and there are those that produce one sound in one position. Either variety is familiar to musicians and listeners around the world. Some musical cultures boast a long tradition of idiophone ensembles. These tend to enjoy high social status in the various cultures

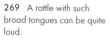

**269** A rattle with such broad tongues can be quite loud.

where they are found, and many of the instruments involved are considered ritual objects.

The African variants of these idiophones are barred instruments made of wood; Indonesia is home to barred instruments made from metal and bamboo, as well as gongs.

## The xylophone

The most familiar idiophone in the western world is possibly the xylophone. Its name derives from the Greek *xylon*, which means wood, and *phonein*, which means sound. Composer and music theorist Carl Orff (1895–1982) introduced the instrument into his musical pedagogy (**271**). The xylophone has wooden bars, arranged by pitch and held on a frame by metal nails or screws. Either the frame expands into a resonating body or, to the same end, under each wooden bar are pipes of appropriately different lengths. The order of the individual bars is modeled on the piano keyboard. Smaller instruments are diatonic (only containing the scale of one particular major key)

**270** By striking a prong, the whole fork is set into oscillation producing a pure tone which musicians use to tune their instruments. Tuning forks come in many different pitches. The most common is probably the A above middle C, which vibrates at 400 hz.

**271** The primary instruments of the Orff instrumetarium are wooden or metal xylophones.

> "All these instruments ... they seem to me like fool's toys. Therefore I am vexed to name them all, and much more to draw them, and most of all to describe them; let me therefore completely omit them here."
>
> Sebastian Virdung on the "wooden laughingstock" (from *Musica getutscht*, 1511)

while larger instruments can be chromatic (containing all the pitches available on a keyboard and thus capable of being played in any key).

The wooden bars are played with felt-headed mallets. Even a beginner can produce a good tone immediately. The pleasantly muted sounds of the bars combine so well that a "wrong note" does not seem to matter much. Very little practice is required to play more than one note at once—for example, a row of parallel intervals. Because of its ease of play and its almost exclusive application in music education, the xylophone (**272**) has a reputation as an instrument of amateurs, and is manufactured in quality ranging from a dimestore toy to better-quality models.

### Something to laugh about?

Barred instruments—precursors of xylophones—date back to at least the 15th century in Europe. The same arrogance that wrote off other instruments that did not fit neatly into a governing standard and ideology also took a dismissive stance toward the xylophone. The attitude of the prominent theorists

**272** The xylophone, as depicted by Marin Mersenne in *Harmonie universelle*; Mersenne takes a similarly dim view of the "wooden laughingstock."

of the Renaissance and the early baroque may be summed up in Sebastian Virdung's description of it as a "wooden laughingstock." His choice of derogatory words probably comes from a German dialect word for "clappers." (Americans are familiar with the modern version of this instrument, the

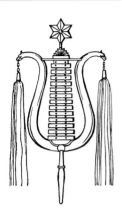

"glockenspiel," from marching bands.) Michael Praetorius also expresses such a patronizing attitude when he labels xylophones "Lumpen Instrumenta," vagabonds' instruments. As with so many other popular instruments, the xylophone appears to have been looked down upon by musicologists and scholars because of its popularity as an instrument of the people. The xylophone was an instrument for folk music (273), and folk music was not considered worthy of scholarly pursuit.

**273** A glockenspiel, very much as is still in use today. The player rests the foot of the instrument in his or her belt, steadies it with one hand, and plays it with the other.

### Interrupted tradition

Like many other Renaissance and baroque instruments that faded into oblivion, the xylophone gradually disappeared, if not from use, then from the historical record. Isolated musical writers of the 18th century described the xylophone as a *psalterium ligneum*, a wooden psalter, or a *strohfiddel*. None of these is a terribly accurate equivalent for the instrument as we know it existed, though all were widespread among the "common people," so the misnomers confirm the xylophone's marginal position.

**274** A genuine half-moon bell originally from Turkey. The many small bells are sounded by shaking and stamping the instrument.

### Revival

In European art music, composers again turned to the xylophone at the end of the 19th century. Some even used it in a few orchestral compositions. Camille Saint-Saëns prescribed it in his *Danse macabre*, Gustav Mahler in his *Sixth Symphony*. In modern compositions with or for percussion, the xylophone often carries the melody line. The chimes (**274**), attached to a keyboard called a celesta, are a similar instrument. They show a close structural kinship with the xylophone but are made of metal instead of wooden bars. They appear in many orchestral compositions, including Tchaikovsky's *Nutcracker* ballet and Bartòk's *Concerto for Orchestra*.

275  An African xylophone.

### The xylophone in Africa

Wooden xylophones are almost as important to African music as drums. With different names and structural variations, the xylophone can be found as a solo and as an ensemble instrument throughout sub-Saharan Africa. Two types may be distinguished from each other: Xylophones with resonators to amplify their volume and those without.

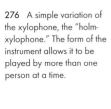

276  A simple variation of the xylophone, the "holm-xylophone." The form of the instrument allows it to be played by more than one person at a time.

The resonators of African xylophones are made from the calabash, round-bellied gourd that is attached underneath the individual wooden bars. Sometimes an opening is cut into the calabash and then closed again with a membrane of adhesive spider web. This changes the typical xylophone sound considerably. Each blow also causes the web on the calabash to vibrate, which creates a quiet buzzing or droning effect.

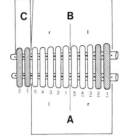

An example of an African xylophone without a resonator is a cross-beam instrument (**276**) in which the sound bars lie across two sticks or beams.

277 A schematic representation of interlocking. Through the interlocking of the basic series, played by player A, and the contrast series of player B emerges a complex sound pattern in which the individual series are no longer recognizable. Player C structures the entire sound pattern by using two tones to reinforce at the octave the basic tones and the contrast row.

## Interlocking

A technique of African xylophone playing that can also be heard on plucked idiophones is the interlocking of two melodic patterns that unite into a single sound. The effect, which is very striking in drum music using rhythmic patterns, is further heightened in xylophone music through the melodic component. These interlocking patterns,

278 Three players at a xylophone.

however, are not melodies in the western sense, but strictly repeated scales that create a whole different from its parts in the listener's ear. This interlocking can be executed by two or more players on a single instrument; they will sit beside each other and strike the xylophone in different areas. Sometimes, as in the Amadinda style in East Africa, this interlocking technique develops a nuance that adds even more depth to the process: A third player will play the two bars at the upper end of the instrument. He strikes either of his two bars when the same note appears an octave lower in one of the two other players' patterns. This player produces a third series of two tones that reinforces the essence of the two basic patterns (**278**).

279   A zanza player.

## Mbira—zanza

As common as xylophones in Africa are plucked instruments with metal "tongues" tied to a resonating chamber—sometimes a gourd, sometimes a hollow wooden box, sometimes a solid wooden block. These instruments are called mbira or zanza and are plucked with the thumb. They are sold in the United States as "thumb pianos." By using both thumbs, the player can play two different patterns and develop an interlocking effect (**279**).

## Metal and bamboo

The music of the Indonesian archipelago is often played on many different kinds of struck idiophones. Most Indonesian instruments are made of metal, with convex arched discs. These are usually set upon sled-like resonators and played with mallets. The same kind of instrument may be built out of bamboo. The bamboo

280  A gamelan orchestra.

variety has a more muted, less penetrating sound that dissipates faster than that of the metal instruments.

## Gamelan

A southeast Asian ensemble of idiophones is called a gamelan. A complete gamelan ensemble or orchestra will include gongs, which are either strung individually or fastened on a box that acts as a resonator; they are played with mallets. Each instrument in a gamelan has a different function.

Like Arabic and Indian music, Indonesian music has developed an ideal melodic model. A group of metallophones play the basic melody, which is elaborated upon by another group. A third group—the gongs—marks characteristic divisions in the

281  The Chinese violin, erh-hu. The instrument's small resonating body is striking. Instruments have spread from China throughout east Asia. The string instruments in the gamelan, however, came to Indonesia from the Arabic world.

rhythm. The fourth group, consisting of string and wind instruments, again elaborates upon the basic melody. Last (but not least), a series of rhythm instruments dovetail their beat patterns into the rhythm set by the gongs and so coordinate the entire ensemble.

Gamelan ensembles (**280**) are in Indonesia what kettledrums and trumpets once were in Europe—symbols of power and influence. In the courtly music tradition of Indonesian villages and cities, gamelan orchestras and their players are highly regarded. Gamelan music may be heard everywhere in Indonesia. It has grown into something of a tourist attraction as an authentic example of regional culture.

### Migrations

The scholarship on individual instrument groups, their relationships and interdependence has proceeded on the ethnomusicological assumption that instruments arrived in the course of diverse waves of migration in different regions of the world and have changed little if at all in their basic structure. One can hear in idiophones from both Indonesia and Africa the so-called "equidistant tonality system" in which the notes of a scale are all a whole tone apart, lacking the occasional half steps found in the major/minor key system. It would be reasonable to infer from such evidence that the instruments moved from southeast Asia to the west.

That the xylophone, as used in jazz and in new music, comes from Africa is obvious. Whether it came to the Americas with the slave trade is less obvious, though certainly, even if the slaves could not bring their instruments with them, they could bring the memory of how to make them and how to play them. The evidence on the precise evolution of American jazz variants of African instruments is inconclusive.

## Marimba and vibraphone

On the marimba and the vibraphone (called
vibes for short), the calabash resonators are
replaced by pipes, which correspond to the
pitch of the respective tone bars. These instruments are generically called marimbaphones
(282), another confusing designation since
some of the African calabash instruments also

282   A European xylophone.

go by this name (though probably not in
their native context, where there is no confusion at all). Since the 1930s a metal marimba-
phone has been produced in the United
States. It had a deeply reverberating tone but
is relatively inflexible. Technology came to the
rescue and an innovation pushed the instrument
into the world of jazz playing. An electrically
operated clapper mechanism periodically
opens and closes the resonating tubes,
producing a vibrato (a slight wavering in
the sound, tremolo). One of the best and
best-known jazz vibes players is Lionel
Hampton (b. 1909), who was largely responsible for establishing the instrument's use in
jazz.

**283** Medieval cymbals. The players hit both cymbals briefly but furiously against one another if they want to sustain the tone.

### The cymbal—Variable in attack

With almost all idiophones—whether they are made of wood or metal or something else—different striking techniques are possible. The sounding bars of a xylophone, for example, can be removed and hit against one another instead of being hit with a stick or mallet. This technique is commonly used for the cymbals (**283**). Cymbals are dish-shaped metal sheets with a nonresonating bump through which a leather hand strap is pulled. Two cymbals are then clashed against each other to produce a loud, reverberating, lingering sound. The cymbal is useful for effectively and loudly setting off important climaxes in orchestral works.

In military music, cymbals often regulate the marching rhythm. In jazz as well as rock and pop music, cymbals are often part of the percussion. A hi-hat is a pair of cymbals operated by a pedal mechanism. Pop cymbals do not look very different from orchestra cymbals but they are mounted on a stand and hit with a drumstick or brushes.

## Classic clappers— Castanets

More than the guitar, the castanets (**284**) are asso- ciated with Spanish folk- lore and Flamenco dancing. These palm-sized flat shells,

which are joined with a rope, take their name from the Spanish word for chestnut. They are clapped rapidly against one another by finger action. Castanet play- ing, which is nowhere near as simple as it appears, is not so much an accompaniment to the Flamenco dance but a part of the dance itself. A skilled Flamenco dancer must also be a virtuoso castanet player.

## Claves and whip

Completely ordinary round wooden sticks used to mark rhythm in dance music are called claves. This Latin designation for keys also appears in the word "clavichord."

Since it is not practical or safe to execute a genuine crack of a whip in an orchestra's per- cussion section, the sound, when called for, is simulated on an instrument made of two iden- tical wooden plates bound together with a cord.

## Shake and scrape

Shaking an object is a completely ordinary pro- cess and yet it is one of the most popular meth- ods of making a rattle (**286**) vibrate. Maracas are hollow balls, origin- ally gourds, filled with grain such as rice or

**284** Castanet playing requires a special finger technique.

**285** A rain stick contains small grains like the maraca, which when turned up- side down trickle from the top down and make a sound like raindrops.

**286** A maraca.

**287** Although this ratchet has only one tongue, it makes quite a noise. Originally used to frighten away spirits, the ratchet is still used as a noisemaker, for example, on New Year's Eve.

millet. These clash when shaken against each other as well as against the wall of the vessel. From Native American traditions, percussionists have adopted the rain stick, a long, hollow tube closed at both ends, also with some type of grain inside. It is played by turning the stick upside down so that the grain will fall, but, to prolong the sound, the stick is fitted with projectiles—nails, sticks, toothpicks—on the inside, which both slow the fall of the grain and create sound as they are tapped by the falling particles.

Another idiophonic playing technique is the scrape. In country and bluegrass music, a thimble is sometimes used to scrape a washboard to produce a rhythmic rasp. With the ratchet, this process is mechanized to some extent. A cog periodically lifts a tongue and causes a loud noise, similar to that of the washboard.

**288** Bells from the *Musica getutscht* of Sebastian Virdung. These four examples have an internal suspended clapper. The bell on the following page has an external clapper mechanism.

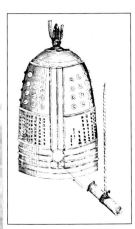

## Bells, bells, bells

Bells are perhaps the most common idiophone in the world. Often associated with the sacred and religious domain, there have always been bells in secular life as well. In either context, they serve as signals—to call the congregation to services or to announce the end of the class period for students.

Cast from bronze or other metals, bells are either struck with an external clapper or set in motion to cause an interior clapper to strike the bell's inner wall. A cluster of several bells—as in a carillon or a bell tower—may be played by pulling ropes. The simultaneous sounding of several bells produces a spectacular reverberant sound.

Bells are believed to be derived from Asia and have spread to differing degrees worldwide. Some peoples believe they convey magical power. In Christian-influenced societies something else resonates unspoken from this idea. Over the centuries bells were rung as a warning before storms and fires. In the face of such an urgent task, the magical aspect receded to the background. Today they are still used as signal instruments and in rituals in different cultures.

**289** Church steeples are often associated with bells. An especially large bell of Cologne cathedral, "the thick Pitter," is sounded only on Christmas and Easter.

Self-Sounding Instruments

# Glossary

Glossary

**Aerophone**: general scientific designation for instruments sounded by air (wind instruments), including the organ.

**Aliquot strings**: resonating strings. These vibrate without being struck, plucked, or bowed.

**Bass bar**: a small piece of wood glued off-center onto the inside of the top of a string instrument in order to increase resonance.

**Bellows**: air reservoir that draws in air and releases it under pressure against a vibrating body.

**Bow**: a flexible wooden rod drawn with hair, used to stroke strings. Bows occur in various shapes and sizes.

**Bridge**: a thin piece of wood placed upright on the top of a string instrument to limit the vibrating segment of the strings and conducting the vibrations to the sound box.

**Chordaphone**: general scientific term for string instruments.

**Diapason**: the relationship between the intervals of strings or pipes that determines their acoustical relationships and how they are played and tuned.

**Fingerboard**: a wooden board-like surface on string instruments against which the strings are pressed to alter their acoustic length. May be fretted or fretless.

**Finger holes**: holes drilled in the pipe wall of a wind instrument; they are closed by the fingers to alter the length of the acoustic column of air.

**Frets**: Divisions on the fingerboard of many string instruments. When the fingers are set against them, they allow the fingers to press the strings at exactly the right point for a given note.

**Idiophone**: general scientific term for self-sounding instruments.

**Intonation**: (1) technical instrumental production of the desired tone at a certain pitch; (2) exact tuning of an organ pipe; (3) trimming of a harpsichord's quills.

**Lip or labium**: (1) in recorders, the flat surface ending on one side with a sharp edge against which the air strikes; (2) on flue pipes of organs, the entire section between the foot (or boot) and the pipe's resonating body.

**Lingual**: the tongue register of an organ.

**Lutes**: general scientific term for all string instruments with parallel strings and a indissoluble connection between the neck and sound box.

**Mallet and sticks**: rods in various forms, especially for striking membranophones and bells.

**Membranophone**: general scientific term for skin instruments.

**Mouthpiece**: part of a wind instrument that is set between the lips. By means of the lips or a reed, the mouthpiece produces the tone.

**Pegs**: in keyboard instruments, metal pins that are turned with a tuning hammer that stretches and tunes the strings; in string instruments (especially in the violin family), wooden pins around which the strings are wound. The pins are set into the peg box below the scroll.

**Pipes**: the sound-producing portion of aerophones. In a narrower sense, the pipes of an organ (labial or tongue pipes). Informal term for flutes.

**Reed**: thin wooden tongue set in motion by blowing; the reed in turn causes the air column of a clarinet or oboe to vibrate.

**Resonator**: in a broad sense, the sound-amplifying segment of a musical instrument, such as the soundboard on keyboard instruments, the sound box on string instruments, and sound horns on wind instruments.

**Ribs or sides**: the side walls between the top and bottom faces of a string instrument.

**Scroll**: the coiled end of the neck on string instruments—in violins typically shaped like a snail.

**Sound card**: the electronic component in computers

# Glossary ... Selected Bibliography

for storing synthetically produced tones that can be played back at any time.

**Sound hole**: the opening in the soundboard or top of a string instrument. On guitars, the sound hole is round; on violins, violas, and cellos, the sound holes are f-shaped (and therefore called f-holes).

**Valve**: a device for shortening or lengthening the air column in brass instruments.

**Zither**: general scientific term for simple chordaphones in which the tone-producing element and the resonator are structurally independent.

## Selected bibliography

While the literature on musical instruments is in some respects plentiful, some of the most valuable discussions of instruments are found in other contexts—embedded in descriptions of music history, theory, and practice; in cultural, sociological, or anthropological studies; and often in art books and collection and museum catalogs, which treat instruments as art objects. This bibliography directs the interested reader toward a sampling of studies on different levels, from the rudimentary to the theoretical. While there may appear to be some repetition among the various encyclopedias, dictionaries, and surveys included here, the history and social role of music and musical instruments is such that different explanations can help stimulate the comparative analytic process. This listing, thus, is far from exhaustive; nor does its selectivity imply a critical value judgment. It merely attempts to give the reader somewhere else to go with his or her musical curiosity. Moreover, let us not forget to go to the libraries and the record stores to find recordings of these instruments in action.

Anderson, Otto Emanuel. *The Bowed-Harp: A Study in the History of Early Musical Instruments*, trans. by Kathleen Schlesinger. London: W. Reeves, 1930.

Bachmann, Alberto. *An Encyclopedia of the Violin*. New York: Da Capo, 1996 (orig. 1925).

Baines, Anthony. *Musical Instruments through the Ages*. Harmondsworth, UK: Penguin, 1961.

Baines, Anthony. *Woodwind Instruments and Their History*, 3rd ed. London: Faber, 1967.

Baines, Anthony. *Brass Instruments: Their History and Development*. New York: Dover, 1993.

Bayo, Martin. *The Message of African Drumming*. Brazzaville, Zaire: P. Kivouvou Editions, 1983.

Beck, John H. *Encyclopedia of Percussion*. New York: Garland, 1995.

Benade, Arthur A. *Fundamentals of Musical Acoustics*. New York: Dover, 1990.

Boyden, David D., et al. *The New Grove Violin Family*. London: Macmillan, 1989.

Campiano, William R., and Jonathan D. Natelson. *Guitarmaking. Tradition, and Technology: A Complete Reference for the Design and Construction of the Steel-String Folk Guitar and the Classical Guitar*. Amherst, MA: Rosewood, 1987.

Chadabe, Joel. *Electric Sound: The Past and Promise of Electronic*

# Selected Bibliography

*Music.* Upper Saddle River, NJ: Prentice-Hall, 1997.

*Classic Guitars of the '50s: The Electric Guitar and the Musical Revolution of the '50s.* London: Miller Freeman, 1996.

Conway, Cecilia. *African Banjo Echoes in Appalachia.* Knoxville: University of Tennessee Press, 1995.

Dagan, Esther A., ed. *Drums: The Heartbeat of Africa.* Montreal: Galerie Amrad African Art Publications, 1993.

Denyer, Ralph. *The Guitar Handbook: The Essential Encyclopedia for Every Guitar Player.* New York: Alfred A. Knopf, 1992.

*Early Musical Instruments* (6-video set). Princeton, NJ: Films for the Humanities.

Geiringer, Karl. *Instruments in the History of Western Music.* New York: Oxford University Press, 1978.

Hayes, G.R. *The Viols and Other Bowed Instruments.* Oxford: Oxford University Press, 1930.

Henley, William. *Universal Dictionary of Violin and Bow Makers.* Brighton, UK: Amati Publications, 1959.

Hipkins, Alfred J. *A Description and History of the Pianoforte and of the Older Keyboard Stringed Instruments.* London: Novello, 1896.

Hood, Mantle. *Atumpan: The Talking Drums of Ghana* (video). Los Angeles: University of California, Institute of Ethnomusicology, 1964.

Hubbard, Frank. *Three Centuries of Harpsichord Making.* Cambridge, MA: Harvard University Press, 1965.

Kaitomi, Margaret J. *On Concepts and Classifications of Musical Instruments.* Chicago: University of Chicago Press, 1990.

Leppert, Richard. *The Sight of Sound: Music, Representation, and the History of the Body.* Berkeley: University of California Press, 1993.

Lieberman, Richard K. *Steinway and Sons.* New Haven, CT: Yale University Press, 1995.

Lindemeyer, Paul. *Celebrating the Saxophone.* New York: Hearst Books, 1996.

Malm, William P. *Music Cultures of the Pacific, the Near East, and Asia,* 3rd ed. Upper Saddle River, NJ: Prentice-Hall, 1996.

Manuel, Peter. *Popular Musics of the Non-Western World.* Oxford: Oxford University Press, 1988.

Myers, Helen, ed. *Ethnomusicology: Historical and Regional Studies.* New York: W.W. Norton, 1993.

Palmieri, Robert, ed. *Encyclopedia of the Piano.* New York: Garland, 1996.

Panum, Hortense. *The Stringed Instruments of the Middle Ages: Their Evolution and Development,* trans. from the Danish by Jeffrey Pulver. London: W. Reeves, 1971.

Pierce, John R. *The Science of Musical Sound.* New York: W.H. Freeman, 1992.

Remnant, Mary. *Musical Instruments: An Illustrated History: From Antiquity to the Present.* Portland, OR: Amadeus Press, 1989.

Sachs, Curt. *The History of Musical Instruments.* New York: W.W. Norton, 1940.

Sadie, Stanley, ed. *The Norton/Grove Concise Encyclopedia of Music.* New York: W.W. Norton, 1994.

Schwartz, Harry Wayne. *The Story of Musical Instruments from Shepherd's Pipe to Symphony.* Garden City, NY: Doubleday, 1938.

Sibyl, Marcuse. *A Survey of Musical Instruments.* New York: Harper and Row, 1975.

Small, Christopher. *Music, Society, Education,* 3rd ed. Hanover, NH: Wesleyan/New England University Press, 1996.

Toff, Nancy. *The Flute Book,* 2nd ed. New York: Oxford University Press, 1996.

Turnbull, Harvey. *The Guitar From the Renaissance to the Present Day.* New York: Charles Scribner's Sons, 1984.

Van der Meer, Ron, and Michael Berkeley. *The Music Pack.* New York: Alfred A. Knopf, 1994.

# Selected Bibliography ... Instrument Museums

Victoria and Albert
Museum. *Keyboard
Instruments at the Victoria
and Albert Museum*, ed.
by James Yorke. London:
V&A, 1986.

Wilson, Sule Greg. *The
Drummer's Path: Moving
the Spirit with Ritual and
Traditional Drumming*.
Rochester, VT: Destiny
Books, 1992.

Instrument museums

## Belgium

### Antwerp
Vleeshuis
Oudheidkundige Musea
Vleeshouwerstraat 38
2000 Antwerpen
Tel. (32)3-233 64 04

### Brussels
Museé Instrumental du
Conservatoire Royal de
Musique
Petit Sablon 17
1000 Bruxelles
Tel. (32)2-512 08 48

### Tervuren
Koninklijk Museum voor
Midden-Afrika
Musée Royal de l'Afrique
Centrale
Steenweg op Leuven 13
3080 Tervuren
Tel. (32)2-769 52 11

## Denmark

### Copenhagen
Musikhistorisk Museum og
Carl Claudius' Samling
Åbenrå 30
1124 Copenhagen
Tel. (45)33 11 27 26

Nationalmuseet
Frederiksholms Kanal 12
1220 Kopenhagen
Tel. (45)33 13 44 11

## France

### Paris
Museé National des Arts et
Traditions Populaires
6 Avenue du Mahatma
Gandhi
75116 Paris
Tel. (33)1-44 17 60 00

Museé de l`Homme
Musée National d'Histoire
Naturelle
17, Place du Trocadéro
75016 Paris
Tel. (33)1-45 53 70 60

Museé Instrumental du
Conservatoire National
Superieure de Musique
221, Avenue Jean Jaurès
75019 Paris
Tel. (33)1-44 84 46 31

## Great Britain

### London
Horniman Museum and
Library
100 London Road
Forest Hill
London SE23 3PQ
Tel. (44)181-699 23 39

Victoria and Albert Museum
Cromwell Road
South Kensington
London SW7 2RL

### Oxford
Ashmolean Museum of Art
and Archaeology
Beaumont Street
Oxford OX1 2PH
Tel. (44)1865-27 80 00

# Instrument Museums

Pitt Rivers Museum
University of Oxford
South Parks Road
Oxford OX1 3PP
Tel. (44)1865-270927
University Museum
Parks Road
Oxford OX4 3PW
Tel. (44)1865-27 29 50

## Germany

### Berlin
Museum für Völkerkunde,
Staatliche Museen Berlin,
Preußischer Kulturbesitz
Lansstraße 8
14195 Berlin
Tel. (49)30-830 12 26

Staatliches Institut für
Musikforschung, Preußischer
Kulturbesitz,
Musikinstrumentenmuseum
Tiergartenstraße 1
10785 Berlin
Tel. (49)30-254 810

### Bochum
Museum Bochum
Kortumstraße 147
44777 Bochum
Tel. (49)234-910 22 37

### Bremen
Übersee-Museum
Bahnhofsplatz 13
28195 Bremen
Tel. (49)421-361 976

### Halle
Händel-Haus
Große Nikolaistraße 5
06108 Halle
Tel. (49)345-500 900

### Hamburg
Museum für Hamburgische
Geschichte
Holstenwall 24
20355 Hamburg
Tel. (49)40-350 42 360

### Leipzig
Musikinstrumenten-Museum
der Universität
Täubchenweg 2 c-e
04103 Leipzig
Tel. (49)341-214 21 20

### Markneukirchen
Musikinstrumenten-Museum
Bienengarten 2
08258 Markneukirchen
Tel. (49)3742-2 20 18

### Munich
Musikinstrumenten-Museum
im Stadtmuseum
St.-Jakobs-Platz 1
80331 München
Tel. (49)89-233 22 370

Deutsches Museum von
Meisterwerken der
Naturwisschenschaften und
Technik
Museumsinsel 1
80306 München
Tel. (49)89-217 91

### Nuremberg
Germanisches National-
museum
Kornmarkt 1
90402 Nürnberg
Tel. (49)911-133 10

## Italy

### Florence
Museo del Conservatorio di
Musica Luigi Cherubini
Piazza Belle Arti 2
50123 Firenze
Tel. (39)11-88 29 25

### Milano
Museo degli Strumenti
Musicali
Castello Sforzesco
20121 Milano
Tel. (39)2-869 30 71

### Rome
Museo degli Strumenti
Musicali
Piazza San Croce in
Gerusalemme 9A
00185 Roma
Tel. (39)6-701 47 96

### Verona
Accademia Filarmonica
Via dei Mutilati 4
37122 Verona
Tel. (39)45-800 56 16

## Netherlands

### Amsterdam
Tropen Museum
Mauritskade 63
1092 AD Amsterdam
Tel. (31)20-568 82 00

### Den Haag
Haags Gemeentemuseum
Stadhouderslaan 41
2517 HV 's-Gravenhage
Tel. (31)70-338 11 11

# Instrument Museums ... Subject Index

**Rotterdam**
Museum voor Volkenkunde
Willemskade 25
3016 DM Rotterdam
Tel. (31)10–411 10 55

**Austria**

**Salzburg**
Museum Carolino
Augusteum
Museumsplatz 6
5020 Salzburg
Tel. (43)662–84 31 45

**Vienna**
Kunsthistorisches Museum
Burgring 5
1010 Wien
Tel. (43)1–521 77

Museum für Völkerkunde
Neue Hofburg
Heldenplatz
1014 wien
Tel. (43)1–52 17 70

**Switzerland**

**Basel**
Historisches Museum
Steinenberg 4
4051 Basel
Tel. (41)61–271 05 05

Museum für Völkerkunde
und Schweizerisches
Museum für Volkskunde
Basel
Augustinergasse 2
4001 Basel
Tel. (41)61–266 55 00

**Neuchâtel**
Musée d'ethnographie
4 Rue Saint-Nicolas
2006 Neuchâtel
Tel. (41)38–24 41 20

**United States**

**Berkeley**
University Art Museum
University of California
Berkeley, California
94729
Tel. (510) 642-0808

**Bloomington**
William Hammond Mathers
Museum
Indiana University
Bloomington, Indiana
47401
Tel. (812) 885-6873

**Boston**
Boston Museum of Fine Arts
479 Huntington Avenue
Boston, MAssachusetts
02115
Tel. (617) 267-9300

**New York**
Metropolitan Museum of Art
Fifth Avenue at 82nd Street
New York, New York
10028
Tel. (212) 535-7710

**Subject index**

*Numbers in italics refer to
the number of the illustration.*

Accordion 46; *46, 68*
active exchange 28
aerophones 39, 43, 63;
    *68*
aerophones, free 42, 106
African music 11, 26, 27,
    137, 144, 146–148,
    159, 162–163, 166; *2,
    37, 249, 254, 275*
air-sounding instruments *37*
airstream 108–109
al 'ud 149
aliquot strings 130
alpenhorn 11, 126; *3*
*alta musica* 101
Amandinda style 164
ancient instruments 13–14,
    87, 92, 150; *2, 10, 11,
    12, 13, 14,154,175,
    258*
angels *9, 75, 150, 191*
Arabic instruments 78, 90,
    94, 96, 117, 137, 138,
    142; *1, 149, 158, 242*
arpeggione 130, 131
arpichordium 132
aulos 14, 121, 150; *2, 12,
    14, 175*
autodidactic learning 29

Back positive *115*
bagpipes 114, 115, 118,
    121; *194, 195*
balalaika 91; *152*
bamboo 164–165
banjo 85; *172*
barbiton *14*
baroque 45, 65, 82, 102,
    107, 110, 113, 116;
    *214*
barred instruments
    160–161
barrel drum 40
baryton 130–131

# Subject Index

# Subject Index

# Subject Index

organ, Bible Regal *102*
organ, electric (Hammond) *108*
organ, positive *64*
organization of musical instruments *27*
origin of instruments *8–11, 92, 104, 158; 174, 238*
otsuzumi *145–146; 250, 251*
overblowing *119*
overtones *124*

Paired drums *143*
paired strings *90–91*
pedals (organ) *61, 62*
pegbox *78*
pegs *78–79, 87*
percata *21*, see also percussion instruments
percussion instruments *16–17, 148; 252*
pi-pa *146*
piano *41, 45, 46–47, 50–51, 52–54, 72; 61, 70, 71, 75, 82, 83, 84, 85, 86, 116, 118*
piano making *72*
piano playing *97–99, 105*
piano, electric *41; 81*
piano, grand *44–45; 61, 79, 80, 117*
piano, spinet *44, 51*
pianoforte *49*
pins *55, 56*
pipes *13, 121, 131; 12, 13, 16*
pipes, organ, reed and tongue *42, 62, 63; 103, 104, 114*
player piano *51*
plectrum (pick) *22, 47, 55, 94*
pommer *101*
plucking *22, 85ff.*
pochette, see *pocket violin*
pocket violin *25, 130; 36, 227*
prell mechanism *74, 76, 77, 78*

prepared piano *133; 231, 232*
private concerts *51, 267*
production of sound *27*
psaltery *17, 19, 47, 55, 101; 20, 75, 123, 170, 260*
psychological effect *12–13, 14, 16, 59, 91*

Qanun *94, 96; 158*
quena *188*
quill *19, 22, 55, 85; 88*
quill clavier, see *harpsichord*

Raga *97, 143*
rain stick *169, 170*
rankette *129; 225*
ratchet *287*
rattles *29; 43, 239, 269*
rebec *78*
recorder *107–108, 113; 65, 66, 176, 179, 180, 182, 185*
reed (water plants) *13*
reed instruments *106, 119; 24*
register (organ) *62, 63*
resonator *14, 25, 38, 40, 41, 42 , 50, 55, 87, 89, 91, 94, 130, 162–163; 36*
restoration and reproduction *71–72; 11*
rhythm *137, 142–143, 146–147, 163*
ricercar *65*
ritual and religion *12, 13–14, 15, 21, 61, 64, 144–145, 150, 152–153, 159; 175, 249, 287, 289*

Sampling *67*
santur *94, 96, 122*
sarangi *52*
saxophone *25, 120–121, 129; 34, 203*
scheffele *44*
screw plate *87*

scroll *129*
self-sounding instruments *37*
shakuhachi *111–112; 189, 190*
shamisen *90; 147*
shanai *117; 201*
shawm *101, 114, 115, 116*
signals, see *communication*
sitar *90; 148*
skin, see *membrane*
snare drum *40, 141, 148, 149*
social function of instruments *7, 19, 52, 125, 151ff., 161, 165–166; 89, 90, 141, 241, 263, 264*
solo *46, 97–98, 102; 70*
sonata *102, 103*
sound box, sound chest, see *resonator*
sound hole *87*
sound recording *235, 237*
soundcard *66*
soundpost *79; 131*
South American music *26; 188*
spindle (jack) *55*
spinet *92*
spinetregal *131*
Spitzharfe *123*, see also *psaltery*
split (or double) chorus effect *101–102*
squeeze box, see *concertina*
Steinway, piano workshop *116*
stick violin *228*
street musicians *45, 76–77*
string-sounding *37, 38*
strings *16, 17, 27, 76–77, 83–84, 132*
strings, gut *86, 90*
synthesized sound *46, 66,155*
synthesizer *132*

Tabla *103, 143; 248*
tailpiece *78–79*
talent *30–31*

# Index of Names

# Index of Names ... Picture Credits

## Picture credits

# Picture Credits

# Notes

# Notes

# Notes

# Notes

# Notes

# Notes

# Notes